THE DESIGNER'S
HANDBOOK

A QUANTUM BOOK

This book is produced by
Quantum Publishing Ltd.
6 Blundell Street
London N7 9BH

ISBN 1-86160-841-1

QUMDH22

Printed in China by
SNP Leefung Printers Ltd.

THE DESIGNER'S HANDBOOK

Series Consultant Editors:
Stan Smith and Professor H.F. Ten Holt

Quantum
Books

Contents

Designing for print.

History. Procedures: Typeface selection, Casting off, Typesetting methods, Marking up copy, Proofs, Imposition and paste-up.

Designing for print History

he variety of typefaces available to designers today is manifold; designs exist in their thousands. The advent of advanced printing technology in the nineteenth century allowed purely aesthetic considerations to influence type design to a greater degree than had been possible in the 400 years or so since type had been invented. Before the nineteenth century, the form of type was largely determined by the limitations of the printing processes available.

Early type designs were based upon handwriting. In Germany, the Gothic handwriting led to a type which, although distinctive, was not easily legible.

Printing in Italy began in the late fifteenth century, and there the typefaces were influenced by the handwriting used for official or formal documents known as Chancery Italic. It was lighter and more legible than German Gothic. Italian handwriting had more influence on the development of type than the German. Indeed, the style is to be seen today, notably the Bembo face.

These Old Style faces were distinguished by the heavily accentuated serif, a small line, which is triangular in form, used to complete the main stroke of a letter. Another feature is the diagonal emphasis given to the thicker part of curved strokes. This feature is derived from the manuscripts used as models for the type.

In succeeding centuries type became less influenced by manuscripts as the mechanics of printing became more sophisticated, and as paper, ink and type developed. In due course typefaces came to be designed quite independent of the influences of the manuscript.

That part of the development of type which came to be known as the Transitional period found a classic designer in John Baskerville (1706–1775), who contributed greatly to the development of type by the improvements he made to the manufacture of paper, type and ink. Baskerville experimented at length in order to improve the surface of paper by pressing it between hot plates to give it a smooth gloss similar to

what is today known as 'wove'. Experiments with ink produced a blacker impression than that of predecessors, while his type designs tended to be a lighter colour than that of Old Style, with a perpendicular emphasis on the curved strokes and the serifs more horizontal than diagonal.

By the end of the eighteenth century the Modern style, introduced by the Italian printer and designer Giambattista Bodoni (1740–1813) was practised. Bodoni used fine, horizontal : hairline serifs and emphasized the difference between thin and thick strokes, thus following the prevailing artistic vogue for the Classical style.

The Industrial Revolution of the late eighteenth and nineteenth century brought significant technological advances and at the same time a greater and more varied demand for typefaces, particularly in advertising. These new designs were less modest than their predecessors. They were bold and black. Slab Serif or Egyptian types had serifs that carried as much weight as the body of the letter, while the extreme Fat Face types had serifs that were exaggerated and gross.

These latter types and others designed to be more striking led designers to realize that the silhouette of a letterform can be made too bold and consequently self-defeating, as the white spaces within the letters, known as counters, become so reduced that the letterform becomes illegible. A natural development from this was the introduction of Roman types without serifs.

Sans Serif or Grotesque types were developed initially as poster faces but soon came into general usage. Jan Tschichold (1902–1974) laid down the principles of the Modern Movement that used these faces in his book *Die Neue Typographie* (*The New Typography*) which has come to greatly influence much of the design in this century. The German *Bauhaus* school and the *De Stijl* movement in Holland produced geometric Sans Serif letter forms that are still influential, while Edward Johnson and Eric Gill in Britain between the First and Second Wars produced significant designs in Sans Serif.

Venetian Centaur
This typeface shows many traces of its origins in fifteenth-century calligraphy.

Transitional Bell
Transitional Bell has horizontal serifs and vertical curved strokes.

Perpetua
Perpetua, like the other faces in its family, was designed specifically to meet mechanical requirements.

Univers
Grotesque Sans Serif Univers is one of the most popular typefaces today and gives a clear effect.

Type families

Gothic
This elaborate early typeface originated in Germany and was derived from manuscript writing. It is fairly hard to read. It is also known as blackletter.

Old English

Old Face
This typeface was influenced by fifteenth-century Italian handwriting, yet is still in common use today. There is little difference between the thick and thin strokes.

Bembo

Transitional
There is less serif bracketing in this typeface than in Old Face. As its name suggests, it falls between the Old and Modern Faces.

Baskerville Old Face

Modern Face
This was developed from Old Face but has thinner cross strokes. There are hairline serifs and stressed vertical strokes.

Bodoni

Egyptian
This group has serifs which are normally unbracketed and appear slab-like. The form is of an even thickness, and some of the more condensed versions are known as Italian.

Rockwell

Fat Face
This face, developed from modern face, cannot be used for setting text. The thick strokes are very broad, making the letters much wider.

Carousel

Sans Serif
This group of typefaces has no serifs. They are fairly recent, and were originally used for posters, before becoming more widely accepted and used in general printing.

Helvetica

Univers

Univers (**below**), a member of the sans serif family, is one of the most popular typefaces today. It was designed in 1957 by Adrian Frutiger, who took into account the effects obtained when using different printing processes. He produced a complete series of letters of different weights and outlines to cater for almost every purpose.

Typesetting variations
These two letters (**right**) have been set, using photo-composition, in different typefaces. The Helvetica face (**left**) has even strokes, but the bottoms of the Univers strokes (**right**) have deep indentations. These allow for fill-in when printing. Many beginners have difficulty in distinguishing between Univers and Helvetica, but generally Helvetica sets tighter.

Condensed
extra light extra

Univers

Light

Univers

Medium
extra condensed

Univers

Light condensed

Univer

Medium condensed

Unive

Bold condensed

Univ

Univer

Unive

Univ

Light

Univ

Medium

Univ

Bold

Uni

Extra bold

Uni

Univ

Univ

Uni

Uni

Medium expanded

Uni

Bold expanded

Uni

Extra bold expanded

Un

Ultra bold expanded

Un

Designing for print Procedures

The two main problems that designers of type have to face are those of the varying width of alphabetic characters and the difficulties of word spacing. The width of alphabetic characters, or the space allotted to them, is largely dependent on the technical apparatus involved. For instance, a manual typewriter, in order to maintain consistent letter spacing, uses exaggeratedly wide serifs on letters such as 'i' and 'l', while some electric typewriters employ a system of three different character widths. Most typesetting machines use a system of nine different character widths.

In order to overcome the problems of word spacing, early printers, who sought to have both margins of text vertically aligned, resorted to a number of extra signs beyond the 26 characters of the alphabet. They were known as contractions and were used to take the place of abbreviated words.

The letterpress printing process allowed for a system of four different width spaces between words, while technological developments in this century have largely obviated the necessity for such devices. The Modern Movement in type design during the 1920s and the 1930s preferred to use consistently equal amounts of word space, which usually resulted in a slightly ragged margin on the right.

Typeface selection

The evolution of type design does not rest solely on historical precedent, but also on the continuing development of production methods, with typefaces being designed, or re-designed, for specific technological innovations. With the introduction of Linotype and Monotype, the first mechanical typesetting machines, at the beginning of this century, the existing typefaces were remodelled and adapted to the characteristics of the two systems. Linotype produces each complete line as a single piece of metal, whereas Monotype produces individual types and spaces with which to form a line.

An important factor in type selection is the printing process to be used. The early typefaces were designed to be printed on cartridge or other uncoated papers. Thus, when printed on modern, smooth papers, they can often appear too light. It is also the case that modern types, designed to be printed on modern paper, have a more robust appearance when printed on cartridge paper. The typesetting equipment can similarly alter the appearance of a typeface—the photographic method, for example, generally produces a lighter effect.

Reversed type, that is white type on a black or coloured background, usually demands a heavier typeface, as a type with fine lines as an integral part of the design, such as a Modern face or light weight of type, is susceptible to the erosion of the image by surplus ink.

Besides such practical considerations, type selection will be influenced by aesthetic demands. Sans Serif faces, simple and uncluttered, are sometimes more suitable for technical literature, and are also used for children's books, the letters more closely resembling today's handwriting. Serifed typefaces are more suitable for novels and are used by the majority of newspapers.

Tables, indexes and bibliographies, requiring complex typography, are best suited to a typeface with a wide range of weight and italic, such as Garamond or Bembo, while Times is a particularly popular typeface for mathematical formulae, with the typesetting done on Monotype equipment.

Colour and leading are two other important considerations. Each typeface produces its own tone or colour, and this colour is further influenced by leading, which is the insertion of space between each line. With hot metal processes this is done by the compositor using a blank piece of lead to space out the line; in photo-composition the term used is line feed.

Some typefaces have large appearing faces. These are faces with the overall height of the body of the type (the x-height) being large in comparison with the ascenders (the parts rising above the body, as in 'b', 't' and 'd') and the descenders ('g' and 'y'). Conversely, a type with a small x-height and large ascenders and descenders is known as small appearing.

The British typographer Stanley Morison (1889–1967) designed the Times New Roman typeface for The Times newspaper in 1931 with an exaggeratedly large x-height in order to give the maximum amount of legibility, however small the size.

Type sizes are measured in points or millimetres, depending on which typesetting equipment is used. The point system is based upon division of the inch into 72 subdivisions. The choice of metrication or the point system is usually determined by the typesetters and printers involved in producing the work. Line lengths are measured in picas or ems, units of twelve points.

Once a suitable typeface has been selected the copy must be prepared by the designer. It is important that the designer is well acquainted with the subject of the copy, as it will influence any decision on a suitable typographic structure. This will include the size and position of headings, sub-headings, references and captions, and may also involve additional sub-editing after a design has been formulated.

It is a considerable advantage to the designer if the text is typewritten and typed to the same approximate line length as the final form. This procedure will also help to confirm the design of a page or pages, and will allow the designer to make an accurate estimate of the number of lines a manuscript will take up.

Casting off

Estimating the number of characters and lines which a piece of typed copy will occupy in type is called 'casting off'. This is an important process for the design of a book or any printed matter.

An approximation should be made of an average line, each inter-word space counting as a single character. This figure is then multiplied by the total number of lines of manuscript to give the number of characters involved. This figure can be used to estimate the cost of setting.

Printers and manufacturers of typesetting equipment will provide sample alphabets in the various typefaces and sizes they have available. When referring to these samples, particular care should be taken, as some typefaces will alter in size according to whether the setting is carried out on hot metal or using photo-composition equipment.

Sets of tables covering a complete range of typefaces are provided by some manufacturers; these tables—called casting-off tables—will indicate the number of characters in a given line length. Other printers provide alphabet sample sheets containing simplified casting-off tables.

However, it is not generally possible to be entirely accurate when judging the length a manuscript will make in type. It is therefore sensible to allow a five or ten per cent margin of error to the estimate. This allowance should take into account the complexity of the manuscript and the number of words per line once it is set in type, although short lines, hyphenated words or exaggerated white spaces due to words being carried over to the next line will further complicate the estimate.

Typesetting methods
There are two basic forms of typesetting—direct or by means of conversion. The oldest of these two forms is the direct method of hand setting. The first types were individually cast, with the space in the interior of the letters or characters produced by individual punches, each cut to the precise form needed. These tools were known as counterpunches—hence the term counters for the white spaces within characters. Type is still produced in limited quantities for use in this way by type founders, and is therefore generally known as founder's type.

Hot metal composition first became widely used at the beginning of this century when mechanical typesetting machines were first built. These machines assemble the brass matrices needed for a line of text and make a casting for them in molten metal, producing individual slugs of lead. In the case of Monotype there was one slug for each character, while Linotype produced a complete line as a solid piece of lead. These castings, with the character in relief, are used to print the text. These machines are limited to a type size of 14 points for body text.

Because the machine operator cannot reduce the inter-character spacing, kerned characters have been developed for some combinations of letters. A kerned letter is one in which some part of the design over-hangs the body of the type and rests upon the body of a neighbouring letter or space. The italic letter '*f*' is a common example.

Photo-composition is considerably more flexible than hot metal, as the individual characters are projected as light on to photographic film. Text can be set closer together than the original sample alphabet indicates. However, there are some faces, such as Univers, which are best not altered in this way as they were specifically designed to be set across a wide measure.

Other advantages that photo-composition has over hot metal are the comparative ease with which matrices can be produced for variants and complete alphabets, the use of prisms to distort the appearance of type, producing expanded, condensed or italic type as required; the wider range of type sizes available, and, above all, the use of photo-composition type as a matrix for processes such as lithography, gravure and screen printing without an intermediate photographic stage.

Electronic editing and typesetting systems use computers to select and edit information in association with cathode ray tube (CRT) typesetting machines which produce 8,000 characters per second or 300 lines of typesetting per minute. These systems are at their most efficient when used to produce directories or similar large amounts of standard information. These systems are widely used in the United States, and are likely to be increasingly used in the British newspaper business in the near future.

Marking up copy
Instructions from designer and editor to typesetting operators should be clearly marked on the manuscript. Typefaces and line lengths should be marked at the head of each page, while words, lines, headings or paragraphs to be set in a different face should be marked accordingly. In some cases, such as in the tabulation of a chess board or graph where instructions might be especially complicated, it is better to send an accompanying style sheet.

Operators and compositors, who impose or make up the text, are liable to work in different departments of a printing works, and thus manuscript marks should be restricted to the manuscript and lay-out instructions to the lay-out.

Proofs
The first proof (or piece of set copy) provided by typesetters is known as a galley proof, which will have the text set to the correct line length in one continuous column. When correcting galley proofs, the accepted printers' marks should be used. In principle, all editorial alterations and corrections should be incorporated in the manuscript because of the cost of resetting type; however, any late editorial or author's corrections and literal errors should be checked diligently, as changes

after pagination further escalate cost.

The second proof is supplied in page form, and should include proofs of illustrations or artwork. Alternatively, photographic prints, which are called bromides, can be supplied. These are pasted down to form a camera-ready paste-up.

Black and white illustrations do not normally require separate proofs, although they are sometimes necessary for identification when a large number of illustrations appear on a page. Colour proofs are essential, however, both for two-colour (black plus one colour) and for four colour (the full colour process).

Imposition and paste-up

The imposition or assembly of type and illustration can be done either by the compositor, by an independent artwork team or by the designer. If the work is to be printed by letterpress, the printer will assemble the hot metal type with blocks in a rigid rectangular frame, known as a forme. If the printing process to be used is lithography, screen process or gravure film will be imposed. A designer will probably work with paper, producing artwork suitable for a photo-engraver's camera. A stout white card is best used as a base for this, with a grid drawn up in light relief to work to. Rubber cement, adhesive sprays or a waxing machine can be used to stick down the paper as they will not wrinkle it when drying.

Lines, whether for illustration or margins, can be drawn in directly onto the artwork. If the drawing is complicated it can be prepared by the artist to a larger size more comfortable to work with, reduced photographically and then pasted up. This last alternative can be applied to the artwork as a whole, including the typesetting, producing it to a larger scale than is required for the finished product and then reducing it. A scale of one to one and a half, known as 'half-up', is usually sufficient for work up to A4 size.

Instant lettering, or dry transfer lettering, such as Letraset, can be pasted up in the same way. Some photo-composition machines do not carry large enough typefaces for certain headings or displays and instant lettering is a useful alternative.

Halftones do not reproduce particularly well when pasted up. The best quality halftones are those prepared by a photo-engraver, who produces letterpress blocks or photographic film. The position of illustrations in the artwork must be clearly marked, usually by indicating the exact corners of the illustration in pencil, with the dimensions of the illustration. The photograph itself should also be marked up, either on an overlay or on the back of the photograph, although care should be taken not to damage the photograph. Requests for retouching or trimming should also be indicated in this way.

1. Width (units of set)
2. Beard (space for descender)
3. Body (point size)
4. Front
5. Foot
6. Nick
7. Height (to paper)
8. Back
9. Shoulder

Typefaces Some typefaces appear fainter than others when reproduced, and therefore need more spacing or leading. This is determined by the x-height — the height of the lower case 'x' — of the typeface. The difference in size of various x-heights is shown **above**, in four alphabets. The varying x-heights of the letter 'h', set in different faces, are also illustrated. This rectangular piece of metal (**left**) is a piece of type, with the printing surface uppermost, called the face. The block is called the body.

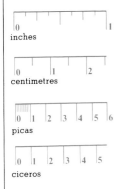

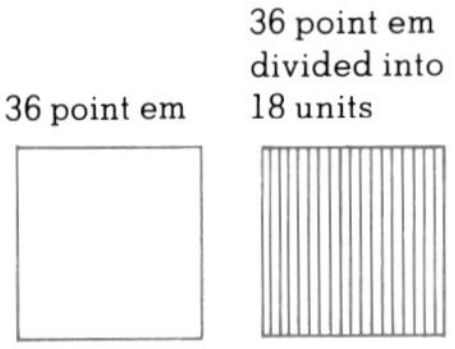

inches

centimetres

picas

ciceros

36 point em

36 point em divided into 18 units

72 point em divided into 18 units

Didot. Britain and America adopted another system. In the European system, the unit of 12 points is called a cicero and in the Anglo-American it is called a pica. The unit system (**left**) is used on photosetting machines. There are usually 18 units to an em, and the size of the unit varies according to the size of the type.

Point sizes Until the eighteenth century, there was no standardized system of type measurement, and each foundry produced a slightly different type. The point as a standard unit of measurement was introduced by Pierre Fournier, a Frenchman. This was developed into the standard European measurement by another Frenchman, Firmin

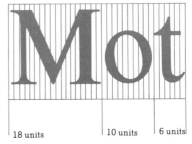

18 units   10 units   6 units

Photon
ABCDEFGHIJKLMNOPQRSTUVWX
abcdefghijklmnopqrstuvwxyz
1234567890 (£$.,–''!?*¼½¾⅓⅔⅛⅜⅝⅞—[]=†/

APS 4
ABCDEFGHIJKLMNOPQRSTUVWX
abcdefghijklmnopqrstuvwxyz
1234567890   £$.,-'':;!?*⅓⅝⅞¾¼⅓½⅕⅜¼⅔⅜⅚⅝⅝⅗⅗

Monophoto 2000
ABCDEFGHIJKLMNOPQRSTUVWXY
abcdefghijklmnopqrstuvwxyz
1234567890(£$.,–'':;!?*¼¼¾ —[]=†/+%&â

Bobst Eurocast
ABCDEFGHIJKLMNOPQRSTUVWX
abcdefghijklmnopqrstuvwxyz
1234567890`ßıêûâéèàùöäüœç

Linotron 202
ABCDEFGHIJKLMNOPQRSTUVWX
abcdefghijklmnopqrstuvwxyz
1234567890 …:;?!()-''——[]/· /æœŒ Æ‡

Linocomp
ABCDEFGHIJKLMNOPQRSTUV
abcdefghijklmnopqrstuvwxyz fifl
1234567890£$.,.:;''!?*—[]†/+%@

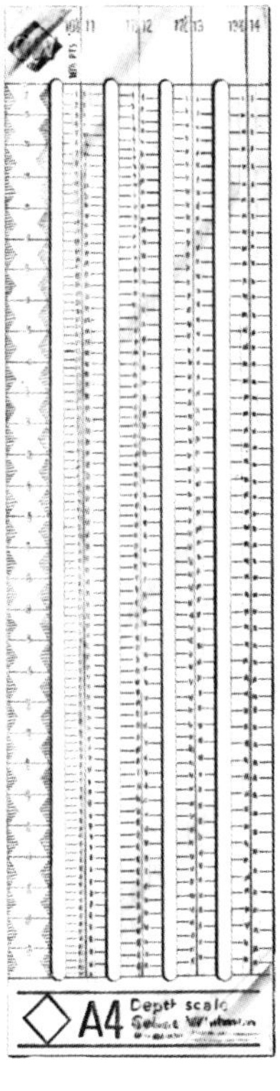

A4

Fine rule
_____

1 point full face
_____

1½ point full face
_____

3 point full face
_____

6 point full face
_____

3 point double medium rule
_____

3 point shaded or total
_____

Broken
– – – – – – – – – –

Fine dotted or leader
· · · · · · · · · · · · · · · · · ·

Coarse dotted
• • • • • • • • • • • •

Type These characters (**above**) set in Monotype are cast on bodies whose width is measured in units. The 'f' set in Bembo, for example, is cast on a 6-unit body but the stem overhangs. The alphabet lengths (**far left**) have all been set in Times typeface on various machines, with very different results. A depth scale (**left**) is calibrated for many different type sizes, in order to show the number of lines needed to fill a given depth. Rules (**above**) are straight printed lines, varying considerably in size.

Typefaces fall into two groups, those having serifs (that is terminal projections on the stems of characters), and those without this feature, which are known as sans serif. In general, serif typefaces are preferable for the easy reading of continuous text, whilst sans serif typefaces are ideal for headings, titles and all the occasions when the text is not of a continuous nature. Both groups are therefore required
Justified

Typefaces fall into two groups, those having serifs (that is terminal projections on the stems of characters), and those without this feature, which are known as sans serif. In general, serif typefaces are preferable for the easy reading of continuous text, whilst sans serif typefaces are ideal for headings, titles and all the occasions when the text is not of a continuous nature. Both groups are therefore required
Range left

Typefaces fall into two groups, those having serifs (that is terminal projections on the stems of characters), and those without this feature, which are known as sans serif. In general, serif typefaces are preferable for the easy reading of continuous text, whilst sans serif typefaces are ideal for headings, titles and all the occasions when the text is not of a continuous nature. Both groups are therefore required
Range right

Typefaces fall into two groups, those having serifs (that is terminal projections on the stems of characters), and those without this feature, which are known as sans serif. In general, serif typefaces are preferable for the easy reading of continuous text, whilst sans serif typefaces are ideal for headings, titles and all the occasions when the text is not of a continuous nature. Both groups are therefore
Centred

Justification Lines of type are treated in one of two basic ways by the printer when setting copy. He can justify, or evenly space, the words to make the lines of the same length. Alternatively, he can space the words equally, making the text unjustified. In this case, he has the choice of ranging the text left, right or centre (**left**). Sophisticated electric typewriters can now typeset, using interchangeable 'golf ball' heads (**right**). The machines are able to justify text on left and right hand margins.

The form typography is to take

The form typography is to take

The form typography is to take

The form typography is to take

The form typography is to take

abcdefgh
abcdefgh
abcdefgh
abcdefgh

Univers Univers Univers

Photocomposition Printers can be far more flexible when they use photocomposition, or film setting, rather than hot metal composition. Characters can be elongated or shortened, and the spacing can be varied by minute amounts.

Casting off

1. Draw a line by the shortest line of copy. Multiply the characters in the line by the lines on the page, add on extra characters.

2. Calculate the number of characters in the entire text, then read a factor figure from the appropriate manufacturer's table.

3. Read this figure against the appropriate pica measure to obtain an exact line character count.

4. Divide this figure into the total number of characters in the text to get the total line count.

5. To cast off from a typesetter's sample, count the characters in 5 lines. Divide this by the lines counted.

6. Divide the total number of characters in the copy by the average number of characters per line to give the line count.

15

Proof correction marks — Instruction to printer	British — Text	British — Margin	American — Text	American — Margin	New — Text	New — Margin
Delete	pen/and ink	ℐ	pen/and ink	ℐ	pen/and ink	ℐ
Delete and close up	pen a/nd ink	ℐ̂	pen a/nd ink	ℐ̂	pen /nd ink	ℐ̂
Leave as printed	pen and ink (dotted underline)	*stet*	pen and ink (dotted underline)	*stet*	pen and ink (dashed underline)	✓
Insert new matter	pen∧ink	and/	pen∧ink	and	pen∧ink	and ⅄
Wrong fount. Replace by character of correct fount	pen ⓐnd ink	w.f.	pen ⓐnd ink	wf	pen ⓐnd ink	ⓧ
Change to italic	pen and ink (underlined)	*ital*	pen and ink (underlined)	*ital*	pen and ink (underlined)	Ш
Change to roman	(pen and ink) circled	rom	(pen and ink) circled	rom	(pen and ink) circled	⅄
Insert space	pen/and ink	#	pen/and ink	#	pen/and ink	Y
Transpose	pen/ink/and	trs	pen/ink/and	tr	pen/ink/and	⊔
No fresh paragraph	pen and ink.⌐ The first	run on	pen and ink.⌐ The first	no ¶	pen and ink.⌐ The first	⊃
Begin new paragraph	and ink.⌐The first	n.p.	and ink.⌐The first	¶	and ink.⌐The first	⌐
Substitute comma	and ink/ the first	⸲	and ink/ the first	⸳̂	and ink/ the first	⸲
Insert single quotation marks	∧pen and ink∧	⁹⁹	∧pen and ink∧	ˇˇ	∧pen and ink∧	⁹⁹

Proof correction

When correcting proofs, it is vital that the standard marks are used. Different countries have their own systems, and, for comparison, a selection of the most important marks have been illustrated (**above**). These marks should always be adhered to, as corrections at later stages are both difficult and costly to make. This galley proof (**left**) has been marked up for literal and other corrections by the editor. The corrections are made both in the text and margin to ensure that the printer understands the instructions. The designer should check the galleys for non-alignment of margins and damaged type, for example. The artwork (**below**) has been marked up for the printer, indicating the typeface, type size and spacing.

In the second quarter of the fourteenth century, illustration broke free from text illumination and panel painting became the rule. The church, state and laity continued to commission both well into the fifteenth century. Artists even acted as propagandists – Uccello, for example, painting for Cosimo de Medici a somewhat one-sided version of the 'battle of San Romano'.

The mid-fifteenth century brought new discoveries in oil painting techniques. Vasari (1511–74), the Italian artist and biographer of painters, credits the brothers Van Eyck with many of them, but it is now known that they were in existence centuries before. The earliest oil painting extant today comes from thirteenth-century Norway. What is certain, however, is that Jan Van Eyck (active 1422, d.1441) perfected an oil medium which revolutionized Flemish painting. It was later taken up by the Italians.

With the invention of movable type and the development of the printing press, illustration moved in two directions – namely works for reproduction and narrative painting. From about 1660, there was an increasing middle-class demand for both.

Scientific progress in glass and lens making during the sixteenth century also influenced artistic developments. The construction of the Camera Obscura by Erasmus Reinhold (1511–1553) for use in solar observation is one major example, for artists later took to the use of the invention to study and more closely observe the subjects of some of their drawings. Both Vermeer (1632–75) and Canaletto (1697–1768) used it to produce closer-to-life paintings. Vermeer's 'Lady with a Guitar' for instance, clearly shows the effect of such study in contour drawing around the folds of the dress.

By the mid-sixteenth century, copper engraving rivalled woodcut as a means of artistic reproduction and in the seventeenth century came the final break with the traditions of Gothic and Renaissance in pictorial art. On the painting front, oils reigned supreme. The decorative title page became a vehicle for engravers, who produced emblematic and allegorical designs, and this attracted many painters to

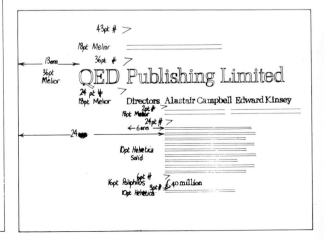

QED Publishing Limited

Directors Alastair Campbell Edward Kinsey

£40 million

Design techniques.

Techniques: Briefing, Roughs, Costing and schedules, Grids, Commissioning text, Photographs, Commissioning illustrations. **Processes:** Copy preparation, Selecting photographs, Sizing pictures, Preparing artwork, Colour correction, Paste-up, Printing, Book production, Flat plans, Binding, Jackets.

Design Techniques

In the production of newspapers, magazines, advertisements, books and related fields, design plays a very important part. Its purpose is always to communicate information in the clearest possible way. To succeed in this task there are two basic factors which have to be considered.

The first is the person or group of people who have commissioned the work. Their aims and ideas must always be borne in mind, and the designer must be prepared for the design to undergo changes before reaching its final form. The second is to be aware of the audience to whom the information is to be communicated. In connection with this, the designer should ask: What is important here? Is the design merely decorative or is it trying to convey the information? If decorative, images are usually allowed to dominate. If informative, the information can be conveyed diagramatically as well as typographically.

Briefing Before the designer can begin, he or she must be given a brief, either by the art director or the client. The idea to be conveyed by the design is clearly stated and design suggestions discussed. It is at this stage that the parameters are set for expenditure and production time.

The designer may be 'in house', that is a permanent member of staff of the company, or working freelance. If the latter, he or she may well be competing with other freelance designers for the commission. But, whether freelance or staff designer, the designer should know how to control a budget.

During the briefing, the designer may simply be given an overall figure to be broken down as he or she sees fit, or a budget in which each component has been costed. Sometimes the designer may be asked to propose his or her own. It is particularly important in the case of a freelance designer that the budget includes a realistic costing of his or her own time. Once a budget has been agreed, it has to be observed.

In competing for a job, a designer must be able to inspire the prospective client with confidence; after all, the client will be paying and authorizing the designer to spend money in the client's interest. How the designer does this depends on who is present at the briefing. The language should be clear, simple and precise; technical language should only be used in discussion with someone who understands it, like an art director. Designers should show flexibility in attitude; sticking rigidly to preconceived ideas could mean that they might lose the job.

The designer should also be prepared in other ways for the interview. He or she should always bring along examples of past work to show their range and approach, or to illustrate ideas. It is also useful to have a notebook and pocket calculator, and even a cassette recorder, if it is likely that complicated technical requirements are to be discussed.

Most important, the designer should be sure to clarify all points, in order to proceed to the next stage with confidence. For instance, if text is to be used, the designer should find out who is to supply it and when. If questions are left unasked, problems are bound to occur. It is helpful to draw up a list of questions beforehand; such an exercise will prepare the designer mentally and pinpoint areas of doubt. The client will not have confidence in a designer who does not ask the right question at the right time.

A designer trying for a commission should be careful to present himself or herself in the best possible light. This applies in the realm of personal appearance as well as in the preparations advised above.

The responsibility of accepting or rejecting a commission lies with the designer alone. But a decision should be made in the confidence that the designer will not let down the client at a later stage. Once the work has been accepted, the client will be paying for it and will naturally expect that the designer will keep to the contract.

Roughs After the briefing the designer goes ahead to produce roughs. A rough can be anything from an outline simply indicating an idea, to a finished rough. The kind of rough produced depends on who is going to see it. An art director is usually able to understand more from an outline, or at least ask the right questions about it, than, say, a salesman. Roughs can be prepared in any medium, although most usually in pencil, felt-tipped pen or crayon. It is best to use pencil to show detail and typography.

The roughs show the designer's approach to the subject. He or she may have decided upon a visual solution, in which case a variety of images or perhaps one strong one have to be selected. The designer also has to decide how many artwork and photographic subjects to use and where, as well as whether they will be in full or two colour, black and white, or a mixture.

A typographical solution poses different problems. For example, there are several ways of emphasizing a key word or line. It can be put into capitals, or set in italics or bold type. The size of the type can be varied, as can its weight. It is also possible to emphasize a line by altering the spacing within it. These are all solutions to one problem which the designer has to decide between in the context of the overall design.

There is one main problem which has to be faced by every designer and that is how to present material in a new way. The way to meet this challenge, of course, depends upon the designer's own imagination. Design is the art of visual communication and the best way to attract attention and interest is through a new idea which is well executed. Novelty is not the only factor here: it may have impact, but this is easily lost if the concept is not thought out properly or is badly produced.

Taking the concept one stage further can be done at the roughs' stage. A preliminary rough provides a talking point, establishing the general subject area and whether or not there will be a central image, for example, but leaving details, like the image to be used, unspecified. In a typographical design; the designer would not have to decide upon the typeface, but the preliminary rough should show how the headings are set out on the page and what size they will be.

Preliminary roughs are likely to be altered several times, so the designer must be prepared to spend time on this stage of the design. Nonetheless, he or she must be constantly aware of the problems of time and cost effectiveness. For instance, it is often tempting to present two or three alternative solutions to a problem, but this is not always necessary or wise. It is just as well to tell the client beforehand how many roughs, and of what standard, will be prepared.

More time is spent initially on a finished rough, because it more accurately reflects the final version. Therefore changes, if there are any, are usually minor. Once again, the images do not have to be exact, but the type of image, the size and colour have to be shown. The designer must specify whether photography or artwork is to be used, and examples of the photographer's or illustrator's work should be brought to the meeting to give an idea of the style and standard of the finished design.

The finished rough is always presented in a professional way. Mount the design on black card with a black or coloured surround and use an acetate covering to protect it. The text should be indicated by dummy type with dry-transfer (Letraset or Letter-Press) headings, or 'live' (real) typesetting. Live copy, headlines and captions are naturally to be preferred, but are expensive to produce. In choosing what text to use, the designer should consult with the writer so that the illustrative and text material will relate. Even when using dummy text, it is better to use live headings to give some indication of subject matter.

Costings and schedules A designer may be asked at this stage to provide printing estimates for the job, although this is often the function of a production department. He or she must therefore be given the size of the print run by the client. This, plus the complexity of the job, will determine what kind of printer the designer is looking for. Other factors to be considered are time and cost. If the job has to be done very quickly, it is likely to cost more, and is unlikely to be placed with one of the more traditional printing firms. A small printing firm, while possibly less expensive than a larger one, may not have binding facilities, and it will increase the cost if binding has to be done by another company.

If it has not already been determined by a production department, the designer may be required to decide how the job is to be handled technically. First of all, this means that the designer will have to see whether it is better to have the typesetting and origination done by the same company or two different ones. With books and magazines it is standard practice to send illustrations to a reproduction house for origi-

nation including colour separation. The type of printing process must be specified, and in relation to this the printer has to be told whether he is to expect camera-ready copy pasted up by the designer, or whether he is required to do the make-up of the film.

In lithography and gravure, the film of the text and the film of the illustrations have to be put together as one piece for printing; this is called make-up.

When costing artwork origination, it is as well to supply a sample showing any special requirements, such as tints.

In fact, to make an accurate quotation, the printer will need all available information about the job. The designer should therefore draw up a detailed layout, marked with all the basic information necessary for his or her own reference and for the printer. If, however, the job is a simple one, a typewritten specification will do.

The aim of the exercise is to obtain the highest standard of printing at the lowest cost. The designer should therefore get as many estimates as possible, or at least a minimum of three, in order to compare available prices.

The printer should supply a timetable indicating how long his part of the job will take. The designer will key this into the overall schedule, which gives dates for each stage of the production process—from roughs to the passing of final proofs.

Grids Grids are devised for consistency in the production of folded leaflets or anything with pages. A single entity, such as a poster, does not require a grid; a book, on the other hand, does.

A grid will show column depths, picture areas, gutters, margins, trim size, folds, type widths, etc. The designer will use this grid for every page in the book, magazine, or whatever is being worked on, so that consistency is maintained. However, the grid will also be used by editors, illustrators, photographers and printers, and so it is important that the information on it is complete. The grid should not intimidate a designer; some of its restraints can be disregarded if an idea demands it.

In large jobs, such as books, grids are usually printed, but in smaller jobs pencil grids are sufficient. Whether to print the grid or not depends on the number of pages and the printing process selected. A grid, however, must always be accurate.

When a grid is going to be printed, it is good to have two types prepared: one on board and one on transparent layout paper. The board can be used for paste-ups and camera-ready copy. The transparent grid can be used for tracing or for checking the fit of illustrations, although the latter is usually done with a film grid which is more accurate than one on layout paper.

Commissioning text Text is normally the province of the editor, but occasionally the designer may have to commission words. It is the designer's responsibility to supply the writer, via the editor, with the number of lines and the measure to which they should be typed. This saves considerable time in counting or calculating the number of words to see if they fit the grid. It also saves on cutting and resetting time and costs. Designers must beware that their specifications do not impose a rigidity either on the design or the information value of the text.

The text can be the determining factor in a design, especially when what is supplied is 'final', that is it cannot be altered or cut. But this is not usually the case. Before a design is complete the editor often has to cut, add or even rewrite to make it fit. That is why it is essential that the editor and designer work together, so that the final product works from both points of view.

Photographs These can either be specially commissioned from a photographer, or can be bought from picture agencies or museums. The latter often requires the services of a picture researcher. If commissioned, the photographer should be carefully selected; most of them specialize in a particular subject, such as fashion, food or scenic views. Some of them even specialize in certain formats. Once the photographer has been chosen he has to be briefed thoroughly, often in the presence of others who are involved, such as the client or writer.

A photographer usually charges by the day, plus expenses. Expenses cover the cost of film and developing, and the hire of a model, a person to find props, and the props themselves: sometimes the hire of a studio or travelling costs are also included. The designer has to work out what is wanted well in advance, so as not to waste the photographer's time. The designer must specify the format or size of the picture, what its subject is, whether it is in black and white or colour, and what type of atmosphere or mood is wanted. The designer's presence is often required at the photography sessions to supervise them.

The designer should also specify whether transparencies or prints are wanted. Unless large format is involved, the photographer will do several shots of a subject, perhaps varying the lighting or the angle, thus giving the designer a choice of pictures.

If pictures are to be bought in, a picture researcher may be hired to find sources and do the preliminary selecting. The picture researcher works from a brief or picture list prepared by the editor and/or designer. The brief gives the number of pictures to be obtained, whether they are black and white, colour or both, the subject matter, and the cost. It should also specify how much time the researcher has to obtain the material. This is particularly important if pictures from other countries are required.

The rights required for a picture are another important factor. The person who is selling or loaning the picture will want to know in what form, size and country it will appear, so that reproduction fees can be calculated. If the picture is to be used in a book,

sometimes the print run will be requested. Fees are payable on publication and pictures should be returned as soon as possible after use, otherwise holding fees may be charged. These can also be charged if a selection is not made promptly, when the pictures are first borrowed.

Museums will either have the subject required on negative, in which case they will sell the print, or have to arrange for their photographic department to take it. Take care if pictures are on loan: replacement fees can be high. Picture agencies will often supply duplicate transparencies, and as they are not as sharp as the originals, they should be checked for quality.

Commissioning illustrations Like photographers, illustrators specialize in certain subjects or in a particular style. The designer must therefore choose an illustrator according to subject and style; he or she must decide, for instance, whether the subject calls for a diagrammatic, naturalistic or decorative style. Another consideration is working in colour—not all illustrators specialize in this.

Illustrators will quote a figure for a job, based on an hourly rate. Because cost in this area is usually high, the designer must keep a careful eye on the quality of the work. Illustrations can cost a great deal more than photographs, and no designer can afford to accept sub-standard work. A rejection fee should be arranged before hand for work that the designer may not be able to use.

A schedule should be established so that the work is delivered on time. This should take account of time for the inevitable corrections.

The artwork is often drawn larger than the size at which it will be printed: usual sizes are half up ($\times$ 1.5) or twice up ($\times$ 2). If this is done consistently, it cuts costs at the separation stage as fewer camera shots need to be made. Also reduction can make the printed artwork look sharper and clearer. However, there are many illustrators whose technique calls for same size reproduction or enlargement. In this case they will arrange to draw their illustrations same size or smaller.

The designer should see a pencil rough before giving the illustrator the go-ahead. The final version should be on art board or paper; paper is preferable as its flexible surface makes it easier to scan at the reproduction stage.

It must be made clear from the start to whom the finished artwork belongs. Unless it is stated that the client is buying the artwork, it is assumed that the work will remain in the possession of the illustrator, who will also retain the copyright. This can cause problems if the artwork is reused. Commissioned photography, however, belongs to the company or individual who pays for it.

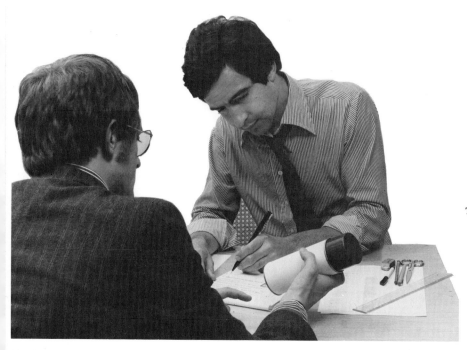

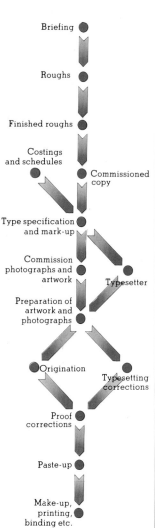

Briefing

Roughs

Finished roughs

Costings and schedules

Commissioned copy

Type specification and mark-up

Commission photographs and artwork

Typesetter

Preparation of artwork and photographs

Origination

Typesetting corrections

Proof corrections

Paste-up

Make-up, printing, binding etc.

Briefings Briefing a designer is the first stage of any job and is extremely important. At this meeting, the client and the prospective designer discuss the design and the image in general terms. The budget and schedule of the project are also discussed and finalized, and the designer will then decide if he or she is able to work within those parameters. If the designer accepts the job, he or she must take careful notes of all details which are discussed, and ask any necessary questions at the meeting. Ideally, the designer should attend the meeting with a list of questions already prepared.

Producing a design This flowchart (**above**) shows the stages in producing a piece of design work. First, the designer is briefed by the client. The designer then prepares and shows roughs to the client, before choosing a final, finished rough. A costing and a schedule are drawn up, and any copy is commissioned. The designer then chooses a typeface and marks up the copy, before sending it to the typesetter, and commissions any photographs or artwork. The illustrations are sent for origination. Finally, when any corrections have been made, the design is pasted up and the paste-up sent to the printer.

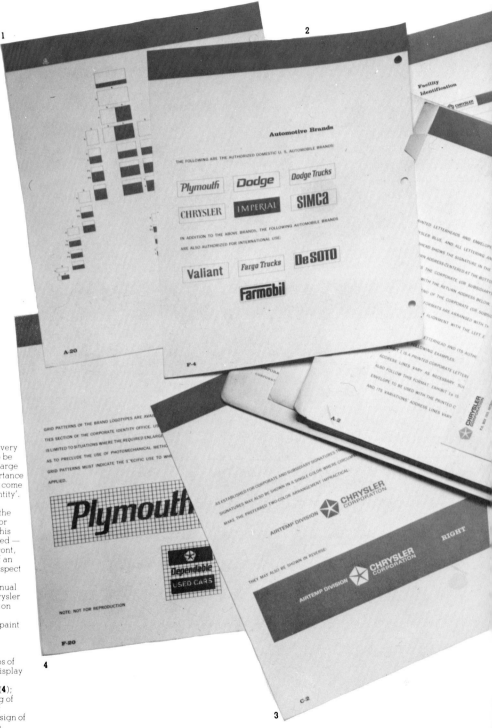

Corporate identity Almost every company wants its identity to be instantly recognizable, and large companies place great importance on this, developing what has come to be called a 'corporate identity'. This is the image which the company seeks to project in the eyes and minds of its clients or customers. The elements of this image can be extremely varied — from a logo used on a shop front, to the detailed application of an image or concept, to every aspect of the company's work. This example (**right**) is from a manual produced in 1962 by the Chrysler Corporation. It gives details on aspects of the company's corporate identity, from the paint design on a truck to the specifications of different letterheads: the design of secondary signs (**1**); the logos of automotive brands (**2**); the display of divisional names (**3**); grid patterns of brand logotypes (**4**); lawn signs (**5**); the packaging of spare parts (**6**); the design of canteen crockery (**7**); the design of trucks (**8**); the wrong ways to reproduce the logo (**9**).

Design processes

When the artwork, photographs and text are in hand and the grids have been drawn or printed, all is ready for the designer to start. It is the designer's job to arrange these elements according to the finished roughs and mark them with instructions for the printer.

Copy preparation The first check is to see if the text fits the allotted space. If not, the editor has to make cuts or additions. Then the designer marks it up and sends it to the typesetter. The typesetter will send back a galley or page proof; he can only do the latter if the designer has supplied him with a detailed layout beforehand. The proofs are checked for misprints (known as literals) and corrections are made.

Selecting photographs While the text is being typeset, the designer can make a final selection of photographs. Photographers usually supply different exposures of the same subject (known as bracketed shots), to give the designer a choice of colour density. Knowing which one is likely to be best reproduced comes with experience; however, the correct exposure usually gives the best result. A slightly underexposed original will tend to give fully saturated colour.

To make sure that the colour is true, the designer has to check the transparencies on a light-box at the correct colour temperature. Transparencies sometimes have a colour scale down one side which shows whether the transparency has kept its colour over a long time. This is particularly important to know when dealing with fine art reproduction. It is also helpful to the reproduction house in matching up the separation with the original.

The designer may wish to incorporate colour in a design where there are only black and white photographs at hand. This problem can be overcome by the use of the four-colour process. The reproduction house can combine colours from the four-colour process with black and white originals to produce one, two and three colour tints, duotones and three colours or sepia. The designer simply has to specify what is wanted within the range that the four-colour process provides.

Photographs should always be checked under a magnifying glass for sharpness of line and scratches. This is obviously important when using transparencies from a picture library, since these have probably been used before, or are duplicates. Damaged photographs can be retouched, but this is specialist work and the cost has to be considered. Permission from the copyright holder must always be obtained before retouching. Retouching is also used in obliterating certain parts of a photograph.

Sizing pictures In reducing or enlarging an image, the designer first has to work out the dimensions required. Then he or she draws the picture, scaled up or down, onto a transparent overlay, which is fixed to the layout over the area which the final picture will occupy. In this way the dimensions and position of the final image are communicated to the reproduction house, and any special requirements, such as cropping (cutting away part of the picture) are made clear. When using a transparency, a projector, which also enlarges and reduces the image, can be used to determine the size of the picture. It will project on to paper an image which can then be traced.

The percentage reduction or enlargement should also be calculated. If it is the same on a number of pictures, they can be put together and photographed at the same time, thus saving on cost. As the controls on reproduction cameras are marked in percentages, it also makes the job quicker. The percentage reduction should be marked on both the layout and overlay. Same size is always 100%.

There may be other specifications which the designer should make—for instance if the image is to be squared, that is, made square; or the designer may wish to use a cut out image, that is, an image with its background cut away. For this it is best to use a transparency with a light background, so that the edge of the image is not dark. The outline, too, should be fairly simple. On a black and white photograph, the unwanted areas are painted out in process white. If an image is 'cut into' another one, it means it overlaps. To do this, the originator must be given very clear instructions as to which picture is cut into which. He should also be given a layout showing how the pictures are to be positioned, with all the dimensions marked.

Preparing artwork Artwork is treated in the same way as photography in preparation for reproduction. Sometimes, however, there is a line overlay which is to be printed in another colour and this has to be dealt with separately. The artwork has a film overlay put onto it; this has registration marks to indicate where it fits. Then the material to be printed in a different colour is drawn or pasted onto the film.

Black and white artwork can be coloured with a mechanical tint. Process colours are chosen from a printer's colour chart; otherwise they can be specially mixed as long as the designer gives the specification.

The designer need only use one overlay to show all the colours needed. This must be marked with lines defining each area of colour. Although this is the easiest method, it is also the most expensive. A cheaper way of doing it would be to have an overlay for each colour.

Colour correction Proofs of illustrations are made up in two ways—either as scatter proofs, which show the pictures at the correct size, but in random order; or the illustrations appear as they would do in the final printed version.

The most important thing to do at this stage is to correct the colour by checking each picture against the original. Colour correction is a matter of correcting the balance. Taking out a colour is easily done by etching it out to a maximum 10% limit. The other factor affecting colour is the inking of the press. The difficulty with correcting this, which can be done during printing, is that all the pictures are affected.

This is also the time to check the proofs for fit, register and damage. The latter can take the form of stains, scratches or broken screens, and the illustration may have to be remade. Although the fit is more important at the printing stage, it should be marked on proof for the printer's benefit.

All the illustrations on one proof sheet are in perfect register when the colour is in the correct position. When it is out of position, they are out of register. The designer should check against the registration marks on the proof, and mark the mistakes to be corrected. On the other hand, an individual illustration on a sheet showing colours that do not register indicates an incorrect fit.

It is important to make sure that the pictures have not been reversed. If they have, a new contact has to be made so that the emulsion is on the other side of the film.

Paste-up There are two types of paste-up: one which the printer simply uses as a guide, and another which is used to shoot final film, known as a camera-ready paste-up.

The first type of paste-up requires the galley proofs to be pasted in position; following this, the printer will produce page proofs, showing the text in the right position, and these can be corrected, albeit expensively.

To prepare a camera-ready paste-up, reproduction pulls called repro are used: film-setting pulls are called galley bromides, hot metal ones are barytas. Corrections, set as words or lines, are stripped into place by hand on the paste-up.

The paste-up for the text film must show the body text, captions, headlines, folios and box rules all in position. The length and thickness of the rules must be specified. It is important to be accurate here to avoid corrections, which are costly at this stage.

Both illustrations and text can be shown on the paste-up used as a guide. However, the camera-ready paste-up should only show type; pictures would have to be masked out. To stick down the type firmly, use an adhesive spray or a rubber solution. These also allow the type to be picked up and repositioned without damage. Double-sided tape can also be used.

If there is type to be printed in a different colour, it should be put on an overlay. This is clearer than making specifications on the paste-up, which can also be done.

Printing The printer puts the text film together with the illustration and sends the designer a final page proof or ozalid, which is a blue-print. This shows how the final product will appear. It also provides the last chance for any correction to be made, but as this has to be done manually, it often proves too expensive to do. In very commercial work, however, pages are sometimes proofed even after the ozalid stage.

Generally, there are two checks to be made at this stage. The first is a reading check to make sure that there is no broken type and that the film is not marked. The second is a check to see that both the text and illustrations are in position.

Plates are made after the ozalids have been returned, and then the job is put on machine. The designer should be present when the printing begins to make sure that the colour is correct. The inking process can be adjusted, but this has to be done right at the start, before too many sheets have been printed—and it should be remembered that presses work very fast!

Book production The production process described above is applicable to books, with the exception of a few factors. The design concept is not presented in roughs, but usually as a dummy book. A blank bulking dummy is ordered from the printer to show the size, quality of paper and binding, and number of pages of the proposed book. Sample spreads (double pages) are pasted inside the dummy to give an idea of how material will be presented in the final book. These can either show real text, headings, captions and illustrations or consist of dummy or nonsense text set in the proposed typeface with picture areas indicated. The latter would demonstrate style and the proportion of pictures to text.

Instead of pasting spreads in the dummy, it can be accompanied by presentation spreads. These are double pages made up or printed on board.

Flat plans Because books are so complex to produce, they should be carefully planned from the start. A flat plan consists of miniature pages, all numbered, which show at a glance how the book is divided into preliminary pages, chapters and endmatter, and where the colour falls. The flat plan can be so detailed as to show type and sketched illustrations on every page, but this is often done for selling purposes only.

Binding Books are usually bound in sections of 16 pages, so the designer has to work in multiples of eight. He or she has to work out where the colour will fall, according to how the book will be printed. It is often too expensive to have colour on every page, so a 'four back two' formula may be used, where a four-colour spread is followed by a two-colour one. This is achieved by printing one side of the sheet in four colours and the reverse in two colours. Folding then ensures that four-colour spreads are followed by two-colour ones.

Jackets These are very important ingredients in selling books. A jacket must attract the eye, at the same time giving the buyer an idea of the content and quality of the book.

A jacket is first presented in rough, that is, drawn and coloured by hand. It should be covered with self-adhesive film laminate to give the impression of lamination. A sample of the trade colour to be used for background or type should also be provided.

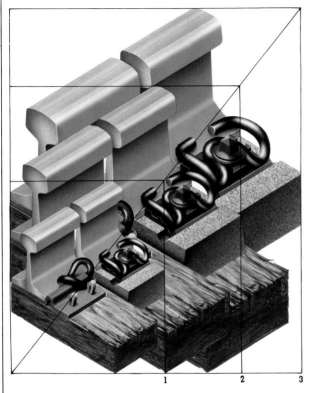

Fitting a picture
1. Fit a transparent overlay to a picture, and then square it up.

3. This will show how much of the picture area can be fitted into the space allowed.

2. Draw a diagonal line on the layout across the area into which the picture must fit, using the overlay as a guide.

4. Any areas on the picture which are to be cropped are shaded out on the overlay. The dimensions are marked on the overlay.

Sizing This illustration (**above**) shows how artwork is often drawn twice as large ('twice-up') (**3**) or half ('half-up') (**2**) as large again, or the same size (**1**), as the required size of the finished piece.

Choosing photographs
Photographs of this subject have been commissioned from a photographer by the designer. Three different exposures have been supplied at different light settings, so that the designer can choose the appropriate one.

Selecting transparencies
Transparencies should not be chosen until they have been checked on a light box (**left**). The special magnifying glass will instantly show up any flaws or scratches on the transparency, which may make it unsuitable for use. This reproduction computer (**right**) calculates the percentage enlargement of a piece of artwork for reproduction. The numbers on the outer ring signify the size of the reproduction required, and the inner ring is the actual size of the illustration. By moving the rings until the two appropriate figures meet, the designer can determine the percentage enlargement.

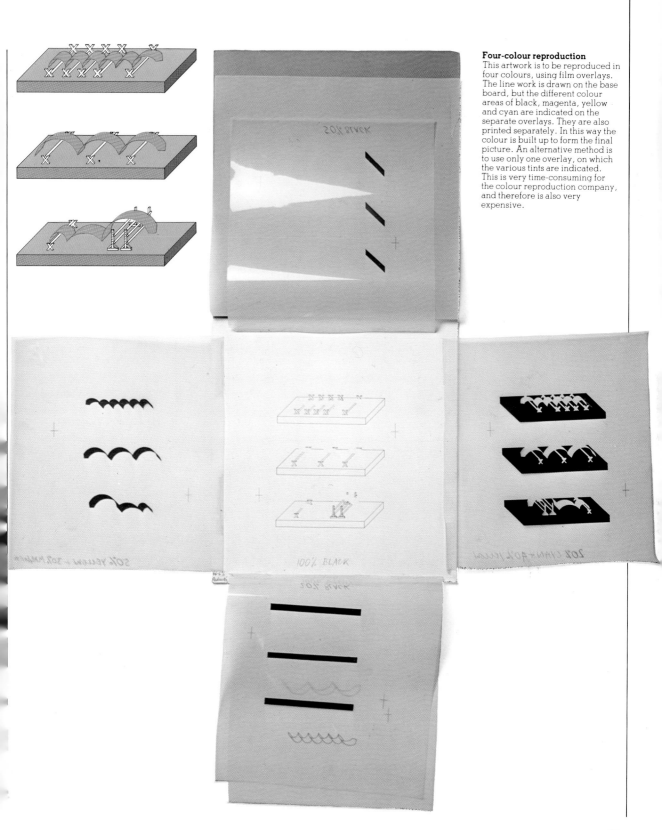

Four-colour reproduction
This artwork is to be reproduced in four colours, using film overlays. The line work is drawn on the base board, but the different colour areas of black, magenta, yellow and cyan are indicated on the separate overlays. They are also printed separately. In this way the colour is built up to form the final picture. An alternative method is to use only one overlay, on which the various tints are indicated. This is very time-consuming for the colour reproduction company, and therefore is also very expensive.

1

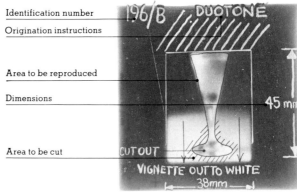

2

Identification number

Origination instructions

Area to be reproduced

Dimensions

Area to be cut

3

4

Marking up photographs This black and white photograph (**1**) is marked up with instructions to the printer. The main image is to be cut out of the rest of the photograph and will be printed without the background. Therefore, the designer must clearly mark on the overlay the dimensions of the cut out, and must also shade, or crosshatch, the background, to indicate the areas not to be reproduced in the final picture (**2**). This 35mm transparency (**3**) has been marked up, before being sent off for origination. The resulting print looks like this (**4**). The smaller black and white photograph (**5**) has been cut-into the large picture (**6**), which has been overlaid with a tone.

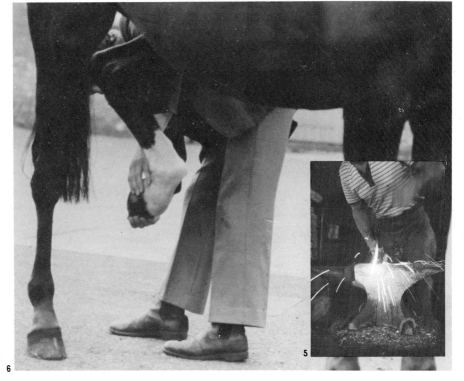

6

5

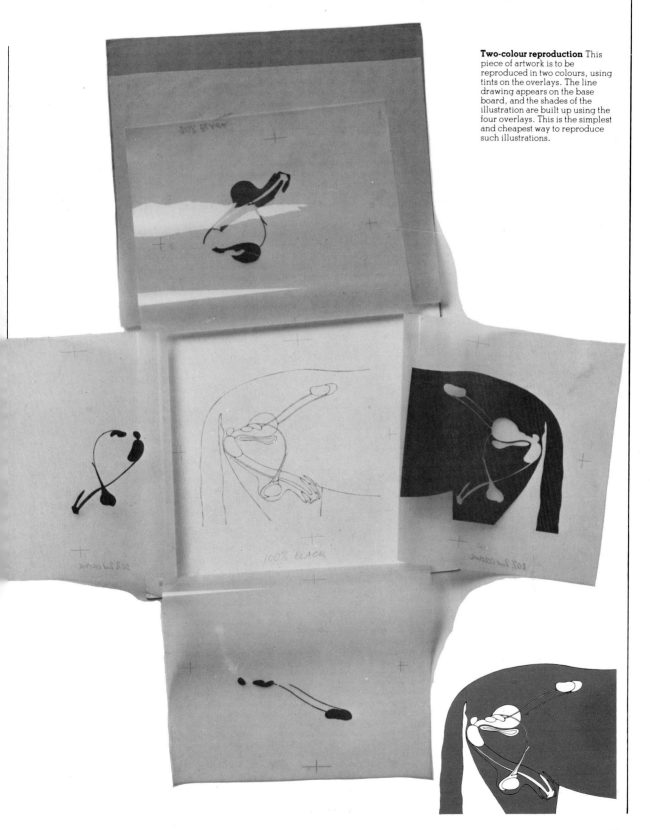

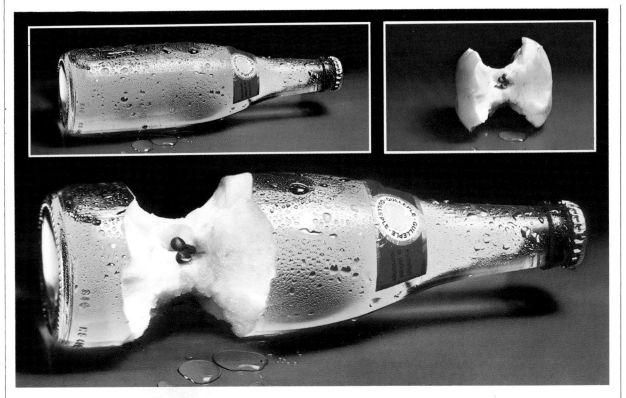

Two-colour reproduction This piece of artwork is to be reproduced in two colours, using tints on the overlays. The line drawing appears on the base board, and the shades of the illustration are built up using the four overlays. This is the simplest and cheapest way to reproduce such illustrations.

Photo-retouching Developments in technology have enabled the art of photo-retouching to be developed to a high degree of sophistication. The picture (**above**) was created from the two inserted shots. Accurate masks have to be used to blot out unwanted areas of the two shots while they are carefully superimposed.

Scatter proofs These proofs (**left**) of illustrations are printed to the correct size but in random order. They must be checked carefully, to ensure that the colour is right, there are no blemishes or spots, and that they are the right size, fit and are in register. They should also be printed the right way round, because it is extremely difficult after this stage to correct a picture which has been reversed.

Grids Printed grids are used if the design job requires consistency and accuracy throughout. They are used particularly in book or leaflet design. The basic grid must show all the essential elements of the book's design, from column depths and type widths, to margins and positions of folios. Very often two types of grid are printed. Transparent grids are used for the rough paste-up, and for tracing off illustrations. Cardboard grids are used for final paste-up and are essential if camera-ready design is needed. **Below** These grids show some of the varying ways in which pages can be designed, using different column and caption widths. This spread (**1**) has a 2-column text and a 4-caption column grid. A 3-column text can have either a 3-column caption grid (**2**) or a 6-column caption grid (**3**). This 2-column text (**4**) has a ½-column caption. This means that the captions can appear in any half column on the grid.

Artist's Handbook

Trimmed page size 192 mm x 246 mm

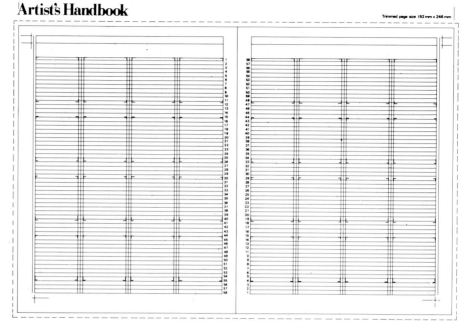

Layouts It is one of the graphic designer's jobs to mark up copy so that the printer sets it in the correct size and weight of type. It is normal for the text, captions, running heads, chapter and cross headings to be set differently. So that the printer or paste-up artist can position the pictures and text correctly, everything must be marked up carefully on the layout. A running head is the heading specifying the chapter; a cross head is a section heading within a chapter. 'Directional' is the term used to indicate the position of the illustration in relation to the caption. A box story is a special feature outside the main text, occurring within its own ruled box.

Running head

Chapter heading

Cross head

Caption

Text

Annotation

Ruled line

Box story

Photograph

Illustration

Directional

Folio number

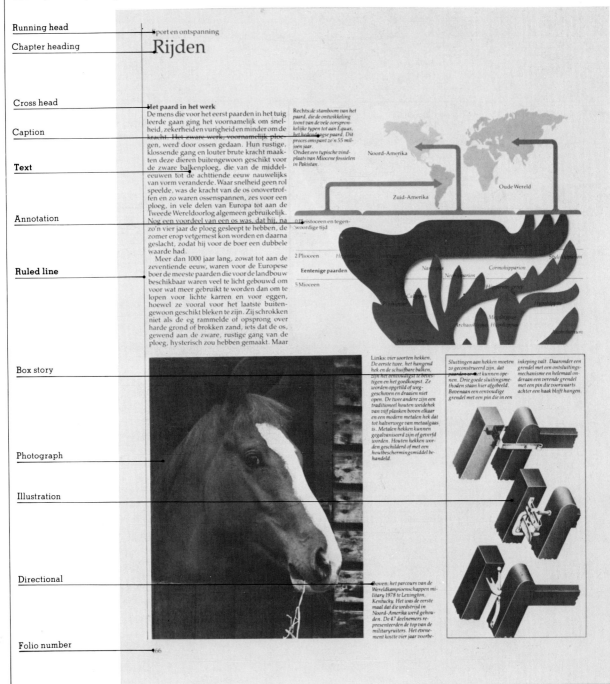

port en ontspanning

Rijden

Het paard in het werk
De mens die voor het eerst paarden in het tuig leerde gaan ging het voornamelijk om snelheid, zekerheid en vurigheid en minder om de kracht. Het zware werk, voornamelijk ploegen, werd door ossen gedaan. Hun rustige, klossende gang en louter brute kracht maakten deze dieren buitengewoon geschikt voor de zware balkenploeg, die van de middeleeuwen tot de achttiende eeuw nauwelijks van vorm veranderde. Waar snelheid geen rol speelde, was de kracht van de os onovertroffen en zo waren ossenspannen, zes voor een ploeg, in vele delen van Europa tot aan de Tweede Wereldoorlog algemeen gebruikelijk. Nog een voordeel van een os was, dat hij, na zo'n vier jaar de ploeg gesleept te hebben, de zomer erop vetgemest kon worden en daarna geslacht, zodat hij voor de boer een dubbele waarde had.

Meer dan 1000 jaar lang, zowat tot aan de zeventiende eeuw, waren voor de Europese boer de meeste paarden die voor de landbouw beschikbaar waren veel te licht gebouwd om voor wat kracht te worden dan om te lopen voor lichte karren en voor eggen, hoewel ze vooral voor het laatste buitengewoon geschikt bleken te zijn. Zij schrokken niet als de eg rammelde of opsprong over harde grond of brokken zand, iets dat de os, gewend aan de zware, rustige gang van de ploeg, hysterisch zou hebben gemaakt. Maar

Rechts: de stamboom van het paard, die de ontwikkeling toont van de vele oorspronkelijke typen tot aan Equus, het hedendaagse paard. Dit proces omspant zo'n 55 miljoen jaar. Onder: een typische vindplaats van Miocene fossielen in Pakistan.

Noord-Amerika
Oude Wereld
Zuid-Amerika

Pleistoceen en tegenwoordige tijd

2 Plioceen
Eentenige paarden
5 Mioceen

Links: vier soorten hekken. De eerste twee, het hangend hek en de schuifbare balken, zijn het eenvoudigst te bevestigen en het goedkoopst. Ze worden opgetild of weggeschoven en draaien niet open. De twee andere zijn een traditioneel houten weidehek van vijf planken boven elkaar en een modern metalen hek dat tot halverwege van metaalgaas is. Metalen hekken kunnen gegalvaniseerd zijn of geverfd worden. Houten hekken worden geschilderd of met een houtbeschermingsmiddel behandeld.

Sluitingen aan hekken moeten zo geconstrueerd zijn, dat paarden er niet kunnen openen. Drie goede sluitingsmethoden staan hier afgebeeld. Bovenaan een eenvoudige grendel met een pin die in een inkeping valt. Daaronder een grendel met een ontsluitingsmechanisme en helemaal onderaan een verende grendel met een pin die voorwaarts achter een haak blijft hangen.

Boven: het parcours van de Wereldkampioenschappen military 1978 te Lexington, Kentucky. Het was de eerste maal dat die wedstrijd in Noord-Amerika werd gehouden. De 47 deelnemers representeerden de top van de militaryruiters. Het evenement kostte vier jaar voorbe

66

Paste up 1. Mark the positions and lines on the board and use as if on a grid.

2. Cut the type to be pasted up square, as this helps to line it up correctly on the boards.

3. Lightly spray the back of the type with a special adhesive which allows it to be repositioned if necessary.

4. Use a T-square or a parallel motion table to ensure that the type is lined up parallel.

Laminating 1. Tape down the leading edges of the subject to be laminated and wipe it over to remove any lumps of glue or dirt.

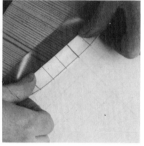

2. Cut the required amount of laminate from the roll, allowing extra for trim. Fold back the backing paper to make crease.

3. Place the exposed underside of the laminate over the end of the subject, with a little overlapping the edge.

4. Firmly push the laminate across the work, using a plastic straight edge. Spread the fingers to keep an even pressure on the laminate.

Types of paste-up On this rough paste-up for a book (**left**), the galley proofs and tracings of illustrations have been pasted down into position by the designer, and the editor has cut or added any lines necessary. On the camera-ready paste-up (**below**), the text, captions, running heads and folio numbers have been accurately positioned and checked. Photocopies or proofs of illustrations are pasted down in their correct positions on the overlay to act as a guide to the printer.

Preparing a dummy book jacket
1. Wrap paper around the dummy and mark folds. Then draw the outline of the jacket, including flaps.

3. Lay the tracing over the colour print or base paper and position dry transfer lettering if used.

5. Make pin pricks at the corners to know where to trim and fold, and then cover the jacket with transparent self-adhesive film.

7. Carefully trim the dummy jacket to size.

2. Make a colour print from the transparency or artwork which is to be used for the cover.

4. Rub down the dry transfer lettering with a blunt burnisher.

6. Score any fold lines to be made on the back of the jacket.

8. Fold the finished jacket around the dummy book.

Finished artwork This finished artwork for a book jacket includes the front and back flap copy. The text and illustrations have been pasted down onto a board in their correct positions, and directions to the printer have been marked clearly on the overlay. The finished jacket is then wrapped around a dummy book (**inset**).

Reproduction processes.

Methods and techniques: Process camera, Dot screen ratios, Colour separation, Line negatives, Colour correction, Screening halftone separations, Transparency quality.

Reproduction processes Methods

Process camera

Development of the process camera has made possible the precise reproduction of artwork in both black and white and comprehensive colour. Pictures, photographs, design, and type can all be reproduced accurately through a variety of printing processes.

There are two types of process camera—the vertical and the horizontal. Both do the same job. They produce finished artwork negatives that can be used for making blocks or plates for printing. The only difference between them is that the horizontal camera can produce from larger originals than the 600mm by 900mm maximum of the vertical models.

The process camera takes a photograph of the artwork under brilliant artificial light and controlled exposure, which gives precise definition to the film. The camera can make reproductions for both types of block printing, line and tone.

Dot screen ratios

Variations of light and shade in a photograph or painting can be reproduced in the printing processes only by breaking up the picture into tiny dots. Ink has a consistent colour weight that shows no gradation of tone. This can be achieved only by converting the negative in the process camera into a series of tiny dots too small for the eye to see.

The process is carried out by a half-tone screen, which is made of two plate-glass sheets each etched with black parallel lines. By placing the sheets together at right angles and laying them 1mm or 2mm above the artwork to be photographed, a picture can be reproduced on the negative which is entirely made up of dots. Each dot reflects the degree of light in its own particular section of the artwork.

The network, of course, shows the exact reverse of what the finished print will look like. In a half-tone print, the darker areas will consist of lots of heavy dots crowded together. Light patches consist of fewer, smaller dots. Grey or shaded areas have dots of different sizes.

Screen levels vary and most are too small to be seen by the naked eye. The mass of colour in the final print shows up only as a gradating tone. For normal graphic reproduction, the screens have between 22 and 70 lines to a centimetre, and these can be detected in the finished work only with a powerful magnifier. The coarser screens, such as those used in newspaper reproductions, have 22 to 29 lines per centimetre, although up to 40 lines are normal when printing on web offset. These screens are fine enough to give good reproduction on low quality paper such as newsprint.

The screen for litho plate printing is usually between 48 and 53 lines per centimetre and this gives excellent reproduction. Quality of paper surface has less importance in litho printing, because the print is taken from a rubber blanket. Very fine screens leave no margin for error in the etching process, and using extra-sensitive plates can be more expensive than using coarser screen.

For very fine quality reproduction with both litho and letterpress printing, a 60-line screen can be used. A vignetted screen gives dots on the finished plate which fade away towards their edges. The negatives are produced by filming the artwork through a contact screen with a line mesh of between 20 and 100 to the centimetre. Vignette screen can be used for monochrome or full colour reproduction. It blurs the grey and shaded areas of the artwork even more than half-tone screen and is ideal for the reproduction of watercolour or fine art printings. The principles of photoprocessing and etching for vignette screen are the same as for half-tone screen, but a vacuum-backed camera is essential for quality results.

Colour separation

Complex colour painting or artwork cannot be printed in a single process. The colour has to be broken down into its basic, primary components and the reproduction made from four separate colour printings.

The process can be used for line or tone plates in conjunction with any of the principle printing techniques—letterpress, litho, screen or gravure.

The artwork is filmed on the process camera through a combination of filters and on to a panchromatic emulsion in order to 'lose' a particular colour on each separate negative. The colour that is lost on the negative is the one that will be printed from it when the negative has been converted into a plate.

The object in colour separation is to produce four plates: one to print the yellow parts of the artwork; one to print the magenta; one for the cyan; and one for the black. Yellow, magenta and cyan are the basic colour printing inks. Black can never be lost from a negative whatever combination of filter is used. In half-tone printing, black provides the under colour and gives tones and gradation to the colour areas.

To separate the yellow component of an artwork it is necessary to photograph the work using a blue-violet filter, which will absorb all the light reflected from all the yellow parts of the original, even where the yellow is only a component of a colour, such as in green. With the yellow light eliminated, the corresponding areas of the negative will appear black and will not be recorded by the photographic emulsion. This is the part which will print from the etched plate. To produce a negative that will print magenta, the original must be photographed through a green filter; and for the cyan negative, it must be photographed through a red filter. The black negative is produced by using no filter at all, or by using a combination of blue-violet, green and red. Choice will depend on the colour bias of the artwork.

For half-tone reproductions, the screen can be introduced at the separation stage and this is called the direct method. In the indirect method, the screen is not introduced until the colour correction stage.

Line negatives

Colour separation process is the same for line printing, but no screen is introduced at any stage. The colour prints solid, but this does not restrict the printer to the basic colours of yellow, magenta and cyan. By overlapping solid colours a wide range of tone can be achieved. Even the shades can be varied by using, say, different tints of yellow and cyan to produce different shades of green.

There is no limit to the range of colours that can be produced by separation for line or tone-printing, but separation of some shades and tones is complicated and expensive. Artwork prepared specially for line printing from colour separations is best done with tri-chromatic colours which match printing ink colours.

Colour separation techniques can be used for printing reproduction of such difficult subjects as delicate watercolour paintings, but, even where special inks are used to attain the accurate tints, some degree of colour correction in the negatives is usually necessary.

Colour correction

Imperfections in printing inks make it impossible to produce perfect colour reproductions without some colour correction. There are two basic ways to correct colour and both methods can be used at the negative or positive stage of the process. One is by the use of skilled hand retouching, the other by photographic masking.

The aim in both cases is the same: to increase or reduce density in a certain area of the negative or plate. Organic dyes of differing strengths are applied by hand to the areas where density is to be increased, or colour reducers are laid over the areas where density is too great in the negative. This technique requires great skill.

Unwanted colour lying under the black printing areas is removed by a method known as UCR, or undercolour removal. This is important because black cannot be filtered away. Unless UCR masking techniques are applied every colour beneath the black printing areas is retained.

There is no need for UCR in slow printing processes, in which each colour is left to dry before the next colour is applied. In such cases, the only value from UCR is in the amount of ink which can be saved.

Fast printing processes on modern machinery make UCR essential in many colour reproductions, or considerable layers of unwanted and unnecessary ink are left underlying the black areas. These colour areas can be removed by photographic masking. The mask is produced from the black separation negative or positive and superimposed upon the respective colour separation negative or positive.

Screening half-tone separations

The angle of the screen through which each separated colour is photographed for half-tone separations must be varied, or the half-tone images will clash, producing a colour which will not only be untrue, but often ugly. Unpleasant, periodic pattern waves called *moiré* are also produced when half-tone separations exactly overlap. Angle variation is normally 30 degrees, but this angle can be adjusted to suit the subject being photographed. The result of the altered angle is to produce dots that do not clash, but form instead small rosette patterns which can be clearly seen under a magnifying glass.

Transparency quality

Always use colour transparencies for half-tone separations; they alone will give the best results. Even so, avoid transparencies from photographs with textured surfaces. These will always produce sub-standard reproductions. So will any original which has an overlying colour bias. It is possible to increase tone in an original that lacks contrast, but do not expect a perfect result from the end product.

Most printing firms lay down strict reproduction requirements. Colour transparencies should meet the following four requirements. There should be a moderate range of density; detail should be clearly shown in both shadows and highlights; thirdly, colour balance should be neutral with no single colour dominating; and finally, there should be sufficient definition of image to stand up to considerable enlargement.

Electronic scanner The electronic scanner is a major technological advance on the process camera. The scanner can perform all the screening processes hitherto carried out by the process camera much faster than with the older methods. Scanners can work with both colour transparency and colour reflection originals and have a steplessly variable enlargement ratio. The four-colour separations made by the scanner are of very high quality. The scanner is made up of two interconnected rotating drums linked to a colour control panel.

Colour chart This printer's colour chart (**right**) indicates the colour values which result when different percentages of the three process colours — yellow, magenta and cyan — are used. A more complex chart could add black to the combinations illustrated. Such charts are very difficult to produce because each colour has to be stripped|in individually; this means that they are also expensive. However, a colour chart is invaluable in determining colour components or selecting tints.

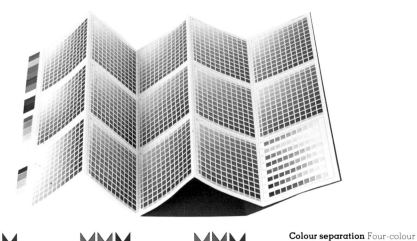

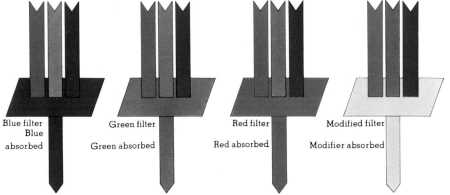

Blue filter
Blue absorbed

Green filter
Green absorbed

Red filter
Red absorbed

Modified filter
Modifier absorbed

Colour separation Four-colour printing uses the basic colours yellow, magenta, cyan and black in varying combinations to reproduce the full colour range of the original. The colour printing process is based on the colour components of light (**above right**) which divide into the 'additive' primaries (red, green and blue) which, when added together, make white; and the 'subtractive primaries' (yellow, magenta and cyan) which are the colours which result when one of the additive primaries is removed. For example, combining red and green without blue gives yellow. The diagram (**left**) illustrates which colours are absorbed when a filter of each of the additive primaries is used. When the blue filter is used, blue is absorbed and red and green reflected, so the colour printed is yellow. When a green filter is used, green is absorbed by the filter, red and blue reflected and magenta printed. If a red filter is used green and blue are reflected, red absorbed cyan printed. To add black, a modified filter is used, which absorbs its own colour and prints black. In the separation process the original is photographed four times, once with each filter, to produce the separation negatives which are proofed in the individual colours (**middle row**). The separation negatives are then rephotographed through a special screen, combining the colours so that the full colour reproduction results (**bottom row**).

Yellow printer

Magenta printer

Cyan printer

Black printer

Yellow proof

Magenta proof

Cyan proof

Black proof

Yellow proof

Yellow plus magenta

Yellow, magenta plus cyan

Yellow, magenta, cyan plus black

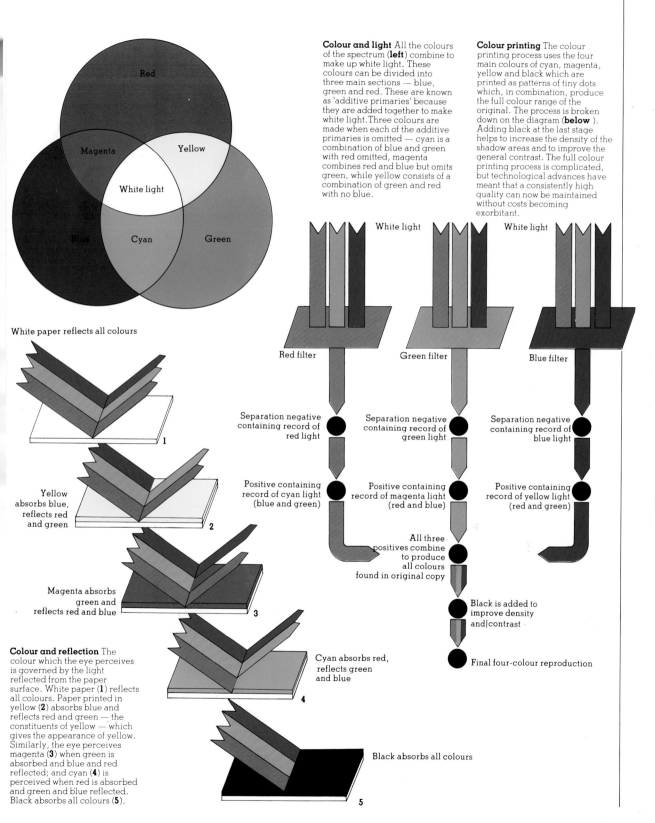

Colour and light All the colours of the spectrum (**left**) combine to make up white light. These colours can be divided into three main sections — blue, green and red. These are known as 'additive primaries' because they are added together to make white light. Three colours are made when each of the additive primaries is omitted — cyan is a combination of blue and green with red omitted, magenta combines red and blue but omits green, while yellow consists of a combination of green and red with no blue.

Colour printing The colour printing process uses the four main colours of cyan, magenta, yellow and black which are printed as patterns of tiny dots which, in combination, produce the full colour range of the original. The process is broken down on the diagram (**below**). Adding black at the last stage helps to increase the density of the shadow areas and to improve the general contrast. The full colour printing process is complicated, but technological advances have meant that a consistently high quality can now be maintained without costs becoming exorbitant.

Red

Magenta   Yellow

White light

Blue   Cyan   Green

White paper reflects all colours

Yellow absorbs blue, reflects red and green

Magenta absorbs green and reflects red and blue

Colour and reflection The colour which the eye perceives is governed by the light reflected from the paper surface. White paper (**1**) reflects all colours. Paper printed in yellow (**2**) absorbs blue and reflects red and green — the constituents of yellow — which gives the appearance of yellow. Similarly, the eye perceives magenta (**3**) when green is absorbed and blue and red reflected; and cyan (**4**) is perceived when red is absorbed and green and blue reflected. Black absorbs all colours (**5**).

Cyan absorbs red, reflects green and blue

Black absorbs all colours

White light   White light

Red filter   Green filter   Blue filter

Separation negative containing record of red light

Separation negative containing record of green light

Separation negative containing record of blue light

Positive containing record of cyan light (blue and green)

Positive containing record of magenta light (red and blue)

Positive containing record of yellow light (red and green)

All three positives combine to produce all colours found in original copy

Black is added to improve density and|contrast

Final four-colour reproduction

1

2

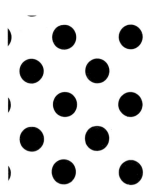

3

Reproduced halftones If a halftone which has been reproduced using a screen (**4**) is enlarged the dot pattern becomes clearly visible (**5**). This shows an enlarged 100 screen dot pattern. If a further enlargement is made, the difference between the dark and light appearing areas can be seen. The dark area (**2**) consists of white dots on a dark background, while the light area (**3**) has black dots and a white background.

Screens A screen must always be used in reproducing a halftone original. The screen is a glass sheet which is engraved with lines which breaks the continuous tone into separate units in a regular pattern. The original is photographed through the screen. The enlarged portion of the screen (**1**) shows that the distance between the lines is equal to the width of the lines themselves. This is a '100 screen', there are 100 lines per inch on the screen. A 55 screen (**6**), with 55 lines per inch, is suitable for producing posters. An 85 screen (**8**) can be used with good quality rotary newsprint. For the best quality of coated papers, it is best to use a 133 screen (**9**). The screen is normally placed so the lines run at 45 degrees to the horizontal. However, the screen can be at any angle, this picture shows the results of setting a 65 screen at 90 degrees (**7**).

4

5

6

7

8

9

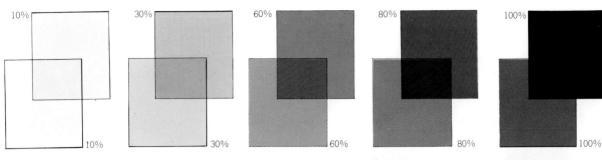

Tints A range of effects can be achieved by combining tints of varying strengths from 10% to 100%. Tints are used in the reproduction of black and white, line or continuous tone copy. On a pale tint it is best to use positive type and on a dark tint reverse type is best. Similar effects can be achieved when colour tints are combined with black and white halftones. The halftone is in shades of black and white. The second colour halftone appears in shades of the second colour and white, while the combined tint and black and white halftone appears in shades of black and colour.

Black and white halftone

Second colour halftone

Second colour tint over black and white halftone

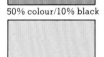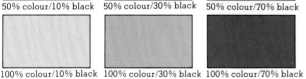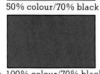

20% colour/10% black   20% colour/30% black   20% colour/70% black

50% colour/10% black   50% colour/30% black   50% colour/70% black

100% colour/10% black   100% colour/30% black   100% colour/70% black

Pantone colour and black selector The internationally recognized Pantone colour system uses eight basic colours, black and white. The selector shows 90 shades of these colours. Using the selector, the designer can choose the colour desired and specify it to the printer using a reference number.

Duotone A duotone is a two-colour halftone made from a black and white original. The original is photographed twice. The first produces a black halftone, the second gives the middle tones in the second colour. The two are combined in varying percentages such as 40%, 60%, and full value.

Black halftone

40% colour halftone over black

60% colour halftone over black

Full value colour halftone over black

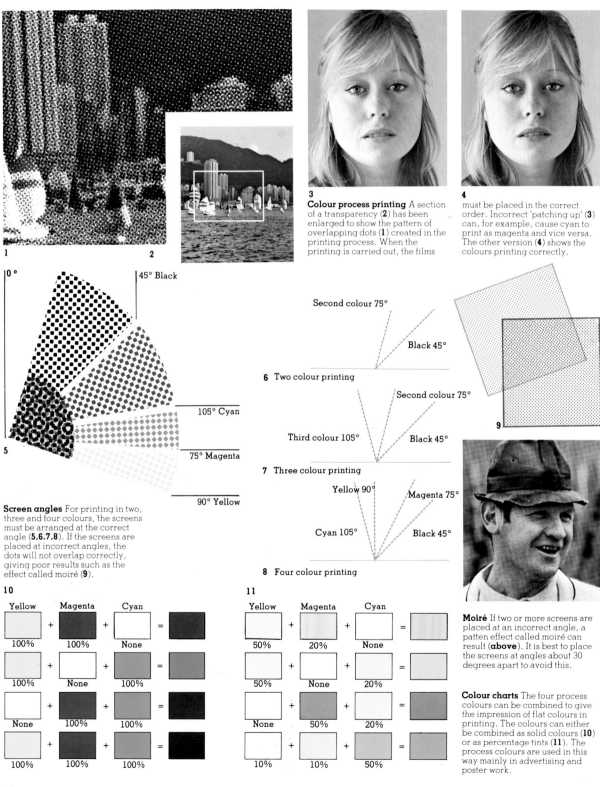

3

4

Colour process printing A section of a transparency (**2**) has been enlarged to show the pattern of overlapping dots (**1**) created in the printing process. When the printing is carried out, the films must be placed in the correct order. Incorrect 'patching up' (**3**) can, for example, cause cyan to print as magenta and vice versa. The other version (**4**) shows the colours printing correctly.

0°

45° Black

105° Cyan

75° Magenta

90° Yellow

5

Second colour 75°

Black 45°

6 Two colour printing

Second colour 75°

Third colour 105°

Black 45°

7 Three colour printing

Yellow 90°

Magenta 75°

Cyan 105°

Black 45°

8 Four colour printing

9

Screen angles For printing in two, three and four colours, the screens must be arranged at the correct angle (**5,6,7,8**). If the screens are placed at incorrect angles, the dots will not overlap correctly, giving poor results such as the effect called moiré (**9**).

Moiré If two or more screens are placed at an incorrect angle, a patten effect called moiré can result (**above**). It is best to place the screens at angles about 30 degrees apart to avoid this.

10

Yellow		Magenta		Cyan		
100%	+	100%	+	None	=	
100%	+	None	+	100%	=	
None	+	100%	+	100%	=	
100%	+	100%	+	100%	=	

11

Yellow		Magenta		Cyan		
50%	+	20%	+	None	=	
50%	+	None	+	20%	=	
None	+	50%	+	20%	=	
10%	+	10%	+	50%	=	

Colour charts The four process colours can be combined to give the impression of flat colours in printing. The colours can either be combined as solid colours (**10**) or as percentage tints (**11**). The process colours are used in this way mainly in advertising and poster work.

Printing processes.

Methods and techniques: Letterpress, Lithography, Gravure, Screen printing, Offset duplicator, Books, Pagination, Folding, Stitching and binding, Translations.

Printing Methods and Techniques

S everal printing processes are available to the artist or designer who needs more than one copy of a finished work. These range from simple sheet-fed, flat-bed letterpress printers still based on the principles applied by the German Johann Gutenberg (1398–1468) when he first printed the Bible in 1450, to the sophisticated oil-and-water techniques of rotary run, web-offset litho.

Study the section on reproduction processes before deciding which method is best suited to your finished work. Take into account the number of copies required—a handful of moderately good quality copies, black and white or in colour, can be run off quickly on instant copy machines using photographic techniques. Where fine quality prints or multiple copies are required, a litho process on high-speed rotary printing may be better.

Letterpress

All processes in which the printing is done from a raised surface, either from type or from a plate, is known as letterpress printing. This is the oldest method of printing. Ink is rolled on to a raised surface and this is brought into contact with the paper.

The Chinese practised this technique, using wood blocks, more than 1,000 years ago. Gutenberg around 1450 was the first to cast type into words and print from them. This method is still used where type predominates, but today the printing surface can be type, or a plate produced by photoengraving.

Pictures are made into half-tone plates, which are locked into a forme with the type. A relief plate is made from the forme, and this is etched or cast in a mould before printing. Some modern methods use thermoplastic material for the printing plates. These are flexible and can be wrapped around the cylinders of a rotary press for rapid printing processes.

Artwork, designs, posters news-sheets and magazines, using mainly type with half-tone illustrations, can be run off on sheet-fed, flat-bed letterpress printing machines, or on rotary presses when there is a big print run.

The type and half-tone plates are laid out to design inside a metal forme, spaced out with lead spacing and rules and borders known as furniture, then locked tightly together.

In the simplest sheet-fed presses, the forme, as it is called, is laid out on the flat-bed and a direct impression taken from it on to the paper. In the oldest technique, used in the platen press, the forme is held vertically and a plate holding the paper is pressed on to it. In other, faster, flat-bed machines, the forme is held horizontally, and the rollers ink the type, then press the sheets down on to it. Two or three colour printing is achieved by repeat processes.

For rotary press printing, a *papier mâché* imprint, known as a flong, is taken from the forme. This is used to cast a curved metal plate, which is subsequently clamped or magnetized to cylinders on the press. By feeding a roll of paper into the machine, a continuous process is achieved with one imprint for each revolution of the cylinders. This method is ideal for the long, high-speed runs necessary for newspapers and magazine printing.

In long-run commercial projects, a number of rotary units can be linked together and the paper fed through continuously, so that three and four colour printing can be done almost simultaneously. Careful control of ink and colour and consistency is vital as all colours are printed wet within seconds of each other. Some machines are capable of printing up to 500ft of paper in 60 seconds. Sheet-fed rotary presses can make up to 6,000 imprints in an hour. These machines are slower than web-offset, but eliminate the cutting process.

Lithography

This is now the most common printing process in use for a vast range of printing from small office duplicators to the large-scale production of newspapers and magazines. It differs entirely from letterpress in that there is no raised printing surface. The process is based on the principle that grease and water do not mix. Image areas are made to attract ink and non-image areas to repel it.

The litho process was first invented by a German typographer, Alois Senefelder, at the start of the nineteenth century. Originally the printing surface was made by drawing onto a polished stone surface, usually limestone, with a greasy crayon. This gave the process its name, from the Greek word *lithos*, meaning stone, and *graphe*, meaning drawing.

Only with the development of high-speed rotary printing and new alloys in recent years has lithography come into its own as the major printing process. Litho plates are now made of a variety of materials, all thin and fairly strong, such as zinc, aluminium, plastic, paper, copper, and chromium. Before each impression, the plate has to be dampened, then inked. Non-image areas are coated with glue to prevent the ink fixing there. The most popular material for litho plates is aluminium, which is strong, light and economic to use.

Complex colour designs and artwork can be excellently reproduced by offset litho printing. Litho inks are grease or fat based—both of which are repelled by water. In the reproduction process, described in the previous chapter, plates are produced which attract ink to the image areas, and repel it from the non-image areas.

The plates are then fitted to the cylinders of a rotary press. A dampening roller applies a solution of water, gum arabic and acid to the plate. A second roller applies ink. Water, clinging to the non-image areas, repels the ink. The imprint is taken by a rubber offset sheet, which finally reproduces the whole design in ink on the paper. The offset rubber sheet is used to protect the delicate surface of the plate from abrasion by the paper. Offset litho machines are available as small office duplicators or as machines large and complex enough to produce a complete book in full colour.

Gravure

This is the reverse of the letterpress printing process—the imprint is not made from a raised surface but by a pattern of small cells recessed into the printing surface to different depths. Each cell is filled with ink, which is then transferred to the paper. Because the cells can be of varying size and depth, variable amounts of ink are transferred to the paper. Depth of the intaglio cells varies from 0.0001mm to 0.4mm in the shaded areas. Considerable depth of tone and colour gradation is possible within these limits.

Very good colour printing results can be obtained with gravure printing, and it is used successfully for a wide variety of reproduction, from newsprint to fine art, for magazines and packaging, floor tiles, wallpaper and decorative laminates.

Three main sorts of cell structure are used in the process. In the first, cells of equal area are cut to differing depths. The second is inert half-tone gravure, in which both the depth and area vary. The third is electro-mechanical engraving, in which a diamond stylus engraving head, operated by an electro-scanner, cuts out pyramids of varying depth and area. In some processes a laser beam is used instead of a diamond stylus.

Gravure is an expensive, but high-speed process used largely for commercial projects. Artwork or designs are etched on to cylindrical copper plates for gravure printing. Carbon tissue, a sensitive gelatin transfer medium, hardens on the cylinder when exposed to light. Ferric chloride is used to etch the image—the depth depending on the thickness of the hardened gelatin. Fine grading can be achieved, and the technique leaves an image etched below the copper surface, and it is this that retains the ink. The etched cylinders are locked into a gravure rotary printer beneath an impression cylinder. This has a hard rubber surface which forces the paper down on to the etched cylinder, leaving an inked imprint.

Gravure is commonly used for packaging, advertising, and some magazine printing. It is also widely used on textiles, cellophane wrappers and vinyl wallpapers, floor tiles and postage stamps.

Screen printing

The use of photographic stencils and developments in ink technology has made screen printing one of the lowest cost methods of reproduction. Printing from stencils is the oldest known form of reproduction, and prehistoric cave dwellers used the principle to decorate cave walls in Gargas, Southern France. They left behind centuries-old hand prints, made by outlining the hand with colour. Even the printers of the Gutenberg bible, which was printed by letterpress, used stencils to guide their colour outlines.

In screen printing, stencils are held in place by a tightly-stretched piece of nylon, organdie or metal mesh, or a piece of weave silk—the method which gave screen printing its common name of silkscreen.

Knife-cut stencils are used in screen reproductions, usually for artwork that has been hand-drawn, but most screen printing today is now done with photo-stencils. These are reproduced on plastic-backed, highly transparent film, which can resist certain inks.

The photo-stencil can be produced by direct or indirect photographic methods. Direct photostencils are made when a screen mesh, coated with light-sensitive emulsion, is laid in direct contact with the artwork. Emulsion is hardened by light in the non-image areas and the image details are washed out with water. Indirect photostencils have to be exposed, washed out, then developed before the stencil is fixed to the screen.

Screen printing can be used on long, high-speed runs, and gives good colour reproduction. It is excellent for designs and hand-drawn artwork.

Offset duplicator

Small accurate copying machines are now common office equipment and are adequate for the reproduction of limited circulation material where sophisticated finished results are not essential.

Pre-sensitized plates of paper, aluminium or plastic are coated with light-sensitive material. These take photographic images of prepared positive or negative copies. These are used to print single-tone reproductions. This system is ideal and inexpensive for sales lists, meeting agendas and factory forms, or wide circulation memos.

Books

The flat-bed cylinder press on which an impression is taken by a roller pressing paper down on to a horizontally held forme is the most common method used for book printing. The paper is turned over for a second printing. Colour books can be produced by running the paper through two or more units. Sheet-fed and web-fed processes are both used.

Fine art books, in which high-colour reproduction is required, are better produced on rotary gravure presses. The system is more expensive, but essential for top quality results.

Pagination

When printed paper has to be folded and then cut after impression, pagination is critical. Each page must be positioned correctly in the flat-bed forme or on the rotary cylinder before printing begins, and this applies equally to sheet-fed or web-fed presses.

Placing the pages in correct position is known as

imposition. To work out the page planning on a flat-bed forme, printing a simple four-leaf sheet, take a sample sheet and fold it right to left. Then fold the top edge to the bottom. You now have a folder of four leaves, giving eight pages when printed on both sides. Number them one to 8 in correct order. Open out the sheet and you have the correct imposition for the pages. The principle can be extended to 16, 32 and 64 page combinations. Before printing begins make a dummy of each section to give yourself an accurate sequence for page imposition. When folding the dummy, draw dotted lines along the folds which are to be cut.

Folding
Almost all folding is done by machine—it is cheaper by far than hand folding and is more accurate. Plan folders with care. Never use thick paper for more than eight folds. With map folds or double folds, make allowance for the folded-in pages being slightly smaller than the outside ones. Make sure there is a minimum margin of 0.25mm. A smaller margin will magnify any faults, for example if the paper does not fold completely squarely.

Stitching and binding
Thin magazines and booklets can be stapled together. This is the simplest and least expensive method of binding. Lay the finished folders one inside the other and open at the centre pages, then staple through the spine. This is known as saddle-stitching. It has the advantage that the finished booklet will open flat for easy reading.

Books that are more than 0.25mm thick should be side-stitched. Place the folded sections on top of each other, numbered from one to the end, and drive stitches through the margin at the spine. Tie, or clinch, the thread at the back. When planning folders to be side-stitched, allow an extra 3mm on the margin at the spine end of the folder, to give room for stitching. Side-stitched books do not lie open like saddle-stitched books, but side-stitching is a more secure method of binding.

Perfect threadless binding is done without stitching. As with side-stitching, allow extra width on the margin at the spine end. Folded sections are then laid together in correct order. Trim off the back; fold; paste with glue and fix direct to the cover. Use a fairly stiff paper or board for the cover.

Translations
Text is often shorter when translated from a foreign language and this presents problems when the illustrations are to be kept. Avoid any overprints in books which are to be published in more than one language—these can send costs rocketing. Use single colour for the type whenever possible to avoid block changes, and when text falls short, it is always cheaper to add more words than to put in extra blocks.

Gutenberg's Bible This extract (**left**) is from the Bible which is generally considered to be the first important work to have come from Gutenberg's press. It is also named the 42-line Bible because each page was divided into two 42-line columns. Another name was the Mazarin Bible — after the French politician Cardinal Mazarin who discovered a copy in his library in Paris and drew attention to its religious and typographical significance. Gutenberg's Bible holds an important place in the history and development of European printing. Completed around 1455, it was the earliest book printed from moveable types which had been cast in moulds, a process that is still used today. The characters were of equal height in a type derived from handwritten Gothic script, probably resembling the best handwriting of the time. It was printed in ink on handmade paper.

Making prints In relief printing (**1**), raised areas of wood or metal are inked and paper is then pressed on to them. Intaglio printing (**2**) is when lines are incised into a block. The paper absorbs any ink in the lines. For planographic printing (**3**), the design is drawn in grease which retains the ink. Stencils attached to a screen or mesh are used in screenprinting (**4**).

Letterpress printing methods The simplest letterpress machine is the platen press (**5**). When the platen opens, the vertical forme is inked by rollers. When it closes again, the paper is pressed against the inked surface. The sheet-fed rotary press (**6**) will print single sheets of various sizes. The speed at which the machine prints can be regulated. The type forme in the flatbed cylinder press (**7**) lies on a flat bed. Inking rollers pass over this and a rotating pressure cylinder presses the paper against the type.

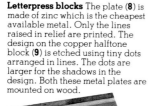
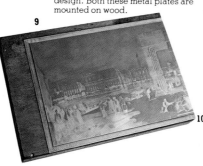

Platen press

Sheet-fed rotary

Flatbed cylinder

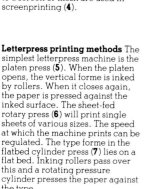

Letterpress blocks The plate (**8**) is made of zinc which is the cheapest available metal. Only the lines raised in relief are printed. The design on the copper halftone block (**9**) is etched using tiny dots arranged in lines. The dots are larger for the shadows in the design. Both these metal plates are mounted on wood.

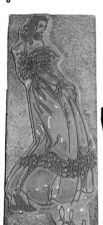

Typesetting The illustrations and type to be printed are locked into place, with leads for spacing, by hand (**10**) or by setting machines.

A flong is then made of the relief design on the flat forme. A curved metal plate cast from this is fitted on the printing cylinder (**11**).

47

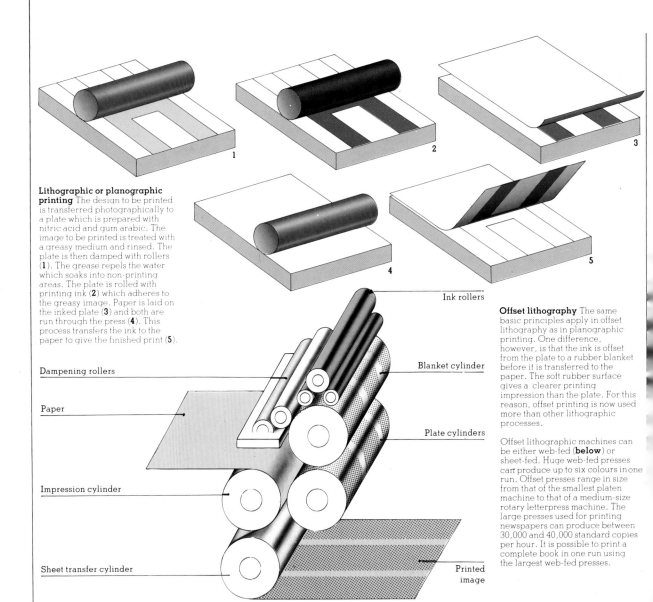

Lithographic or planographic printing The design to be printed is transferred photographically to a plate which is prepared with nitric acid and gum arabic. The image to be printed is treated with a greasy medium and rinsed. The plate is then damped with rollers (**1**). The grease repels the water which soaks into non-printing areas. The plate is rolled with printing ink (**2**) which adheres to the greasy image. Paper is laid on the inked plate (**3**) and both are run through the press (**4**). This process transfers the ink to the paper to give the finished print (**5**).

Dampening rollers

Paper

Impression cylinder

Sheet transfer cylinder

Ink rollers

Blanket cylinder

Plate cylinders

Printed image

Offset lithography The same basic principles apply in offset lithography as in planographic printing. One difference, however, is that the ink is offset from the plate to a rubber blanket before it is transferred to the paper. The soft rubber surface gives a clearer printing impression than the plate. For this reason, offset printing is now used more than other lithographic processes.

Offset lithographic machines can be either web-fed (**below**) or sheet-fed. Huge web-fed presses can produce up to six colours in one run. Offset presses range in size from that of the smallest platen machine to that of a medium-size rotary letterpress machine. The large presses used for printing newspapers can produce between 30,000 and 40,000 standard copies per hour. It is possible to print a complete book in one run using the largest web-fed presses.

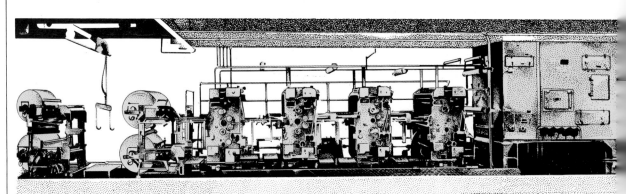

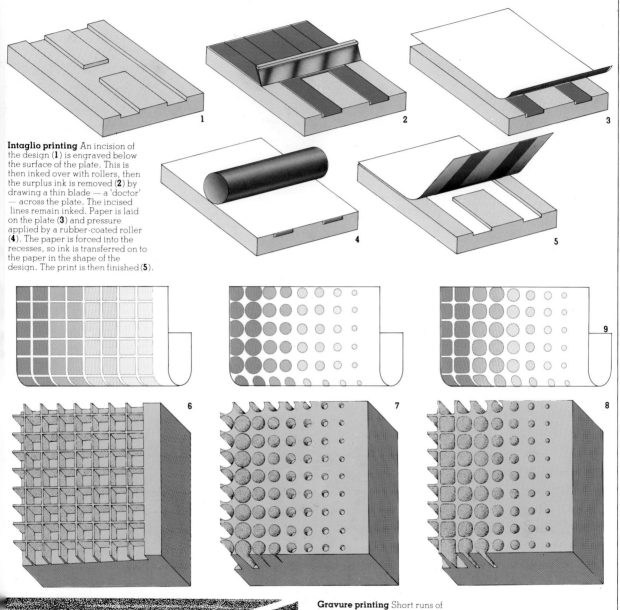

Intaglio printing An incision of the design (**1**) is engraved below the surface of the plate. This is then inked over with rollers, then the surplus ink is removed (**2**) by drawing a thin blade — a 'doctor' — across the plate. The incised lines remain inked. Paper is laid on the plate (**3**) and pressure applied by a rubber-coated roller (**4**). The paper is forced into the recesses, so ink is transferred on to the paper in the shape of the design. The print is then finished (**5**).

Gravure printing Short runs of high quality illustrations are printed best by using conventional gravure plates (**6**). The cells on this plate vary in depth but have equal surface areas. In variable area variable depth gravure (**7**), the size as well as the depth of the cells varies. This is suitable for long run periodical printing. Variable area direct transfer gravure (**8**) is widely used for packaging and textiles. As the image areas do not vary in depth, limited tones are available. In the enlarged detail (**9**) it is clear that an image printed in gravure consists of thousands of dots.

Lithographic printing 1. The surface of a photographic plate is coated with a light-sensitive medium spread with a whirler.

4. The plate is developed and thoroughly rinsed with water. The clean surface of the plate is then protected with gum arabic.

Gravure printing 1. The design is transferred from a plate on to carbon tissue which is exposed to light on the gravure screen.

4. Ferric chloride is used to etch the cylinder. Grading and tones are produced depending on the thickness of the gelatin resist.

2. The plate is exposed with a negative image in a vacuum frame and then treated with an emulsion developer.

5. Any flaws in the plate must be corrected carefully by hand. The plate is then firmly fixed around the plate cylinder.

2. Gelatin hardens in the tissue, when it is exposed in contact with the plate. The tissue is then mounted on the cylinder.

5. The etching incises lines below the copper plate's surface. The first proof is taken and any small corrections are done by hand.

3. The developer dissolves the unexposed coating leaving a gum surface on the main printing areas and lacquer on the image.

6. The plate is treated so the ink is attracted to the image. This is finally offset on to a rubber blanket and then on to paper.

3. Paper backing is removed to develop the tissue. Areas of gelatin remain as an acid resist.

6. The cylinder is usually 'chromed' to give it a durable surface. Then it is mounted on the rotogravure press.

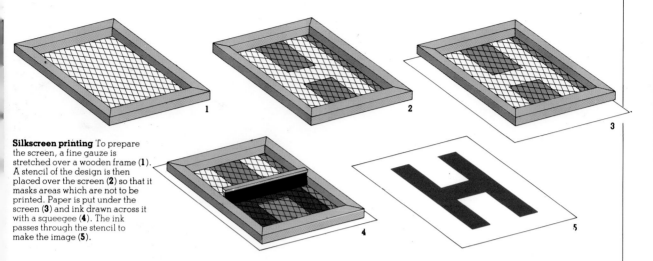

Silkscreen printing To prepare the screen, a fine gauze is stretched over a wooden frame (**1**). A stencil of the design is then placed over the screen (**2**) so that it masks areas which are not to be printed. Paper is put under the screen (**3**) and ink drawn across it with a squeegee (**4**). The ink passes through the stencil to make the image (**5**).

7. The cylinder is rotated in a trough of printing ink so that the surface is covered. Excess ink is removed by a flexible blade.

Silkscreen printing 1. The stencil is taken from a film positive and retouched manually. The screen is coated with emulsion.

3. Any excess emulsion must be scraped from the screen. Paper is next positioned accurately under the screen ready for printing.

5. Ink is drawn across the screen with a rubber squeegee. The screen is pressed down by the squeegee, so the ink prints.

8. In web-fed gravure, the paper is fed continuously through the press, passing between the etched plate and impression cylinders.

2. The positive is exposed to ultra-violet light. Then the emulsion is washed from the image area using cold water.

4. The screen and the paper must be properly aligned in the frame before the printing process, known as 'pulling', can begin.

6. The wet print is carefully removed. It is stacked in a drying rack in front of a fan or blow heater.

51

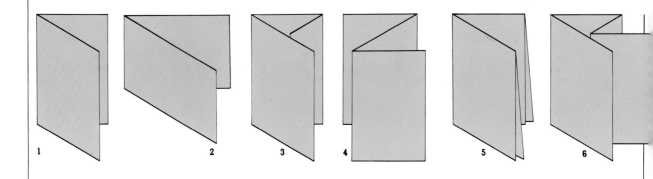

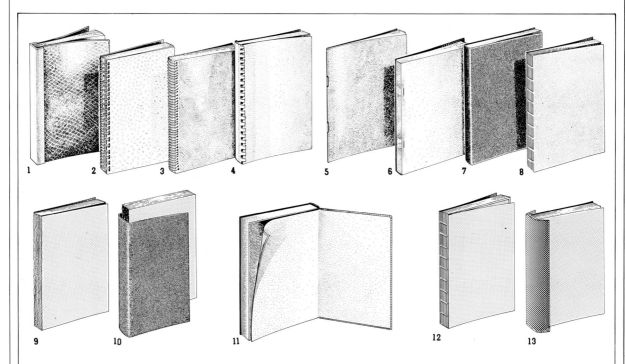

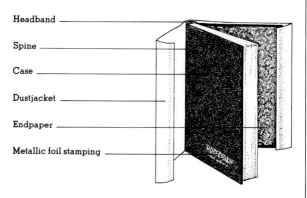

Bookbinding methods In mechanical binding (**1**), a plastic gripper slides over the spine to hold the pages and covers tightly together. In open-flat mechanical binding (**2**, **3**, **4**), the pages and covers are punched with holes. A wire or plastic coil through these holes then binds the pages firmly. For saddle-stitch binding (**5**), an open book is stapled along the back fold. In side-wire stitching (**6**), wire staples are inserted from the front, about ¼in from the back edge. They are then clinched at the back. For thermoplastic binding (**7**), the pages are trimmed along the back edge. These are bound together with a hot plastic glue. The strongest stitched method is sewn stitch binding (**8**). Pages are sewn together in sections, and then sewn again as a whole book. Edition binding is the most expensive method — 16 or 32 pages are sewn together in sections by machine. The trimmed back edges are coated with glue (**9**). A strip of gauze is then glued to the backbone (**10**) and a cloth cover is prepared. The book is finished (**11**) by placing it in a casing-in machine which pastes the end-leaves and fits the cover. A cheap method of binding used for paper back books is perfect binding. The spine edge is roughened (**12**) so the glue will adhere strongly. A cover is then glued firmly in place (**13**).

Headband

Spine

Case

Dustjacket

Endpaper

Metallic foil stamping

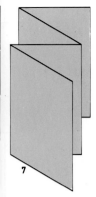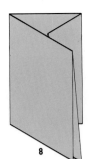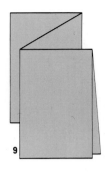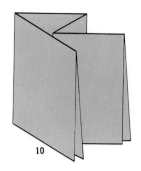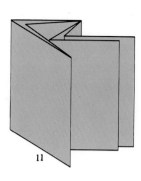

7   8   9   10   11

Imposition and folding

Imposition refers to the position of each page on the printed sheet. The most common impositions are: four page folder (**12**), six page (**13**), eight page — work and tumble (**14**), eight page — work and turn (**15**), twelve page (**16**) and sixteen page (**17**). The numbers on the diagrams indicate the order of the pages when folded. The letters indicate the folding sequence. The dotted lines show where the paper is to be cut. The pile of printed sheets must be held steady by the grippers before they are folded individually. 'Work and tumble' means the sheet is turned over after one side is printed, and the grippers hold the opposite edge. In 'work and turn', the grippers hold the same edge, while the second side is printed.

A four page folder is made by folding the paper once, either across the length (**1**) or width (**2**). Six pages are produced by making a double fold. Two types of parallel six-page folds are regular (**3**) and accordian (**4**). The eight page folder is made by folding paper six times — either one parallel and one right angle fold (**5**), two parallel folds (**6**) or three accordian folds (**7**). Twelve pages are made with one parallel and two right angle folds — regular (**8**) or accordian (**9**). The sixteen page folder is one parallel and two right-angle folds (**10**), or three parallel folds (**11**).

14 Eight page folder — work and tumble

15 Eight page folder — work and turn

12 Four page folder

13 Six page folder

16 Twelve page forme

17 Sixteen page forme

Imposition The term imposition is probably derived from printers constantly repeating the words 'in position'. This imposition (**below**) indicates the layout for one side of a printed 32 page signature. When the sheet is folded and cut, the pages will read correctly.

Design equipment.

Equipment: Pencils and pens, Drawing instruments and equipment, Papers, Knives and sharpeners, Lights and glasses, Dry transfer lettering, Colour selectors, Adhesives.

Graphic design Equipment

A comprehensive range of equipment is imperative for a graphic designer to maintain a high standard of workmanship. Some items are commonplace and have long been standard; others are results of recent technological developments. All are important.

Pencils and pens

Graphite or lead pencils come in up to 17 grades of hardness, while coloured pencils come in ranges of up to about 72 colours. Clutch pencils or lead holders have separate refillable leads which come in various grades of thickness or hardness. For plastic surfaces or film a Chinagraph can be used, while the all-surface pencil can be used on glass.

Pens are as much an essential for the designer as pencils. The dip pen, although old-fashioned, is still used because of its sturdiness and the variety of inks and nibs it will take. The fountain pen takes a smaller range of nibs and most use only writing or non-waterproof inks, although Osmiroid make a model for waterproof drawing ink.

In technical drawing evenness of line is essential and stylo-tip pens with tubular nibs have been developed for this purpose. The barrel pen has a wide range of nib widths and uses an interchangeable nib unit which can also be used for drawing with rulers or stencils. Special attachments are made for use with compasses. The most common type of stylo-tip is the Rapidograph; the Isograph was designed to help overcome problems of drying ink, gives better ink flow and line quality and is easier to maintain.

Felt tip markers produce a thick line and are less hard wearing than fibre-tip pens. They both use spirit or water-based inks, and come in a variety of thicknesses. A newer development is the rolling-writer ball pen, which has the same features as a conventional ball-point pen but which is filled with a water-based ink which flows evenly and smoothly.

Drawing instruments and equipment

A set of drawing instruments is essential for a designer. A moderately small set would include two sets of spring bow compasses, a small radius compass, dividers, ruling pens and an extension bar for drawing larger circles. A beam compass can be used for drawing circles and arcs larger than normal. Among the various attachments for compasses are a lead holder, a ruling pen, a cutter blade and an attachment for a stylo-tip pen.

Ruling pens are designed for producing lines of constant thickness. A standard model has two prongs between which the ink is held. An adjustable screw varies the thickness of the line. Ruling pens, also called drawing or bow pens, mainly use ink, although paint can be used if thinned down to the consistency of ink. The railroad pen has a double nib attachment for drawing parallel lines.

Proportional dividers are used for copying drawings on a smaller or larger scale, and are commonly used by cartographers. A dotting pen draws dotted lines by raising and lowering the pen tip by means of a wheel mechanism; various types of dotting wheels are on the market today.

There are a number of rules, guides and templates a designer will need. The most basic is a ruler, followed by a T-square. By placing the 'T' over the side of the drawing board parallel lines can be drawn by moving the T-square. A plastic scale rule is often used in technical drawings to enlarge or diminish scale, a compositor's typescale for measuring width of type in points, picas, centimetres and inches, and a depth or typographer's scale for measuring type and column depth.

Set squares come in various sizes, as well as adjustable versions; used with a ruler or T-square they produce parallel lines. Parallel rulers and speedliners do the same task. Ellipsographs, by definition, are used for drawing ellipses, as are various plastic templates. French curves are clear plastic line guides designed to provide as many degrees of curve as possible, while flexible curves can be bent to any desired angle.

Drawing boards provide a smooth surface for designers to work on. Wooden boards may require a backing sheet, while a formica covered board is more easily wiped clean. Adjustable models have a drafting head which can be fixed on any position on the board.

Drawing boards can also be adjusted to various angles; some are clamped to a surface and adjusted for any angle, while others adjust to a set number of positions. A drawing stand offers the same flexibility, with counterweights to help hold position and a movable straight edge across the board. The Rotoboard is particularly flexible and is used for work requiring multiple ruling.

Papers

A designer should have a wide range of papers to hand, and in varying sizes. Among those he or she will need are cover paper, a coloured paper for protecting artwork; detail or layout paper for preparing roughs and layouts; tracing-down paper, which has a coloured backing and can be used for tracing a drawing; and acetate paper, used to protect finished roughs or dummy books.

Kodatrace, which is matt on one side and shiny on the other, is used for overlays and particularly for coloured artwork; while transparent adhesive paper is also used for protecting different types of artwork. Cartridge and tracing paper are also indispensable for all types of design work.

Knives and sharpeners

A range of cutting implements are standard equipment. Surgical scalpels are used for fine cutting, and have interchangeable blades, while the craft knife has a larger blade than the scalpel and is used for cutting thicker materials such as stencils or board. A trimming knife also takes various blades and is a heavy duty instrument for all types of cutting.

Scissors are an obvious essential for design work, and a more sophisticated instrument is the parallel cutter with two blades.

A designer should also have a selection of sharpeners, and a sandpaper block is useful for finer sharpenings than are possible with a conventional sharpener.

Lights and glasses

A light box is a necessary piece of equipment for checking the sharpness of transparencies and negatives, for checking colour separation and, in conjunction with a suitable overhead light, for colour correction. A light box provides uniform and colour balanced light diffusion over the viewing surface by throwing a fluorescent light through an opalized perspex or acrylic diffuser on to the glass surface of the box.

A vizualizer or enlarging projector is invaluable for enlarging or reducing an image to an exact size. The image is placed on a copyboard and lit from above—or below in the case of a transparency—and is projected through the lens. The degree of enlargement or reduction is controlled by the movement of the copyboard up or down and by the adjustment of the lens. The image is projected on to the tracing paper on the glass viewing screen, and can then be traced off to an exact size.

Magnifying glasses are especially useful for checking work that has to be enlarged, while a special glass is used for viewing transparencies. A repeat glass is useful for repeating patterns to show how the finished design will look, and is mainly used in fabric and wallpaper design.

Dry transfer lettering

Dry transfer lettering is a fairly recent development now invaluable for rough and finished artwork. Manufacturers of instant transfer products supply a catalogue with examples of the lettering styles, typefaces, sizes, colours and effects available, each with a reference number for identification. They also supply specialized alphabets, such as Greek, Hebrew and Arabic; Roman and non-Roman numerals; architectural and technical symbols; illustrations; textures and tones; rules and borders; lines and transfer tapes; and colour surfaces such as Vinyl and PVC.

Colour selectors

Pantone is a range of products for selecting and matching colours, allowing the designer to control and match colours in all stages of the design, printing and reproduction from the initial roughs to the finished print. There are more than 500 colours available, each with a reference number, and the system is in international use.

The products start with colour and tint overlays in large and small formats, each with a colour guide. There are wide and fine pointed markers and corresponding coloured paper sheets with colour guides to help select and match colours; paper pickers show all colours in numerical order, and the printer's edition gives them on coated and uncoated paper. A colour and black selector gives different amounts of black in combination with 90 of the colours, and a colour specifier is provided to specify inks.

Adhesives

There are a number of adhesives suitable for design work. Rubber gum, applied with a spatula, is a basic stand-by, although increasingly popular are spray adhesives. There are also special aerosol glues for mounting photographs. Among the more specialized adhesives are latex glue for bonding fabrics and fixatives for dry-transfer lettering. Waxers can be used for sticking paper, and other useful items are solid glue in stick form and plastic putty adhesive.

There is also a wide variety of tapes on the market. This includes one-sided and masking tape, double-sided tape suitable for mounting and 'Magic' tape, which becomes almost invisible on application. Gum strip is used for stretching paper in watercolour work.

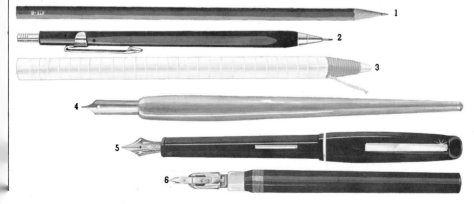

Pencils and pens It is essential for the graphic designer to have a wide range of pencils and pens. The graphite pencil (**1**) comes in up to 17 grades of hardness. The clutch pencil (**2**) is useful as it can be refilled with many leads that are graded according to thickness and hardness. The Chinagraph (**3**) can be used for drawing on both film and plastic surfaces. The dip pen (**4**) is favoured by some designers as it can be fitted with a variety of nibs and takes a wide range of inks. The fountain pen (**5**) takes only a small selection of nibs and inks but the Graphos reservoir pen (**6**) can use a much larger range.

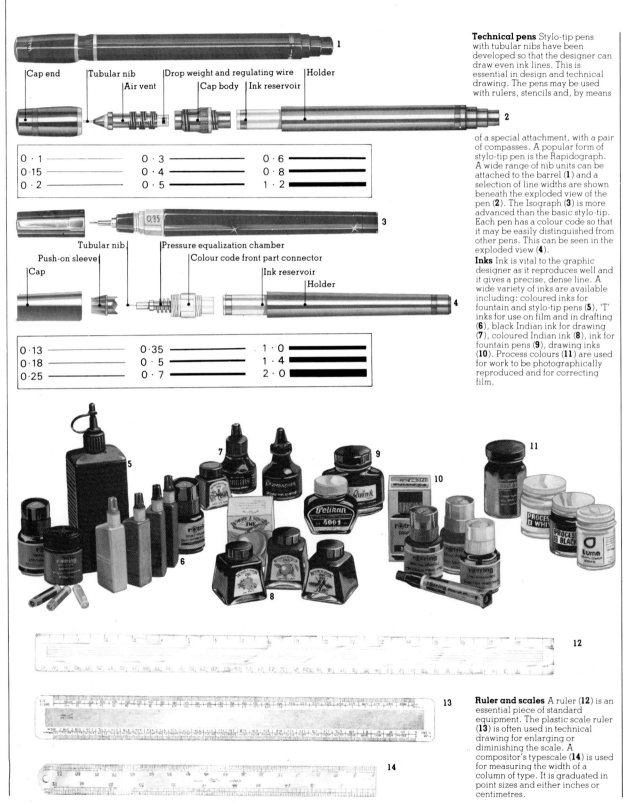

Cap end | Tubular nib | Drop weight and regulating wire | Holder
Air vent | Cap body | Ink reservoir

1

2

0·1	0·3	0·6
0·15	0·4	0·8
0·2	0·5	1·2

3

Tubular nib | Pressure equalization chamber
Push-on sleeve | Colour code front part connector
Cap | Ink reservoir | Holder

4

0·13	0·35	1·0
0·18	0·5	1·4
0·25	0·7	2·0

Technical pens Stylo-tip pens with tubular nibs have been developed so that the designer can draw even ink lines. This is essential in design and technical drawing. The pens may be used with rulers, stencils and, by means of a special attachment, with a pair of compasses. A popular form of stylo-tip pen is the Rapidograph. A wide range of nib units can be attached to the barrel (**1**) and a selection of line widths are shown beneath the exploded view of the pen (**2**). The Isograph (**3**) is more advanced than the basic stylo-tip. Each pen has a colour code so that it may be easily distinguished from other pens. This can be seen in the exploded view (**4**).

Inks Ink is vital to the graphic designer as it reproduces well and it gives a precise, dense line. A wide variety of inks are available including: coloured inks for fountain and stylo-tip pens (**5**), 'T' inks for use on film and in drafting (**6**), black Indian ink for drawing (**7**), coloured Indian ink (**8**), ink for fountain pens (**9**), drawing inks (**10**). Process colours (**11**) are used for work to be photographically reproduced and for correcting film.

5

7

9

11

6

10

8

12

13

14

Ruler and scales A ruler (**12**) is an essential piece of standard equipment. The plastic scale ruler (**13**) is often used in technical drawing for enlarging or diminishing the scale. A compositor's typescale (**14**) is used for measuring the width of a column of type. It is graduated in point sizes and either inches or centimetres.

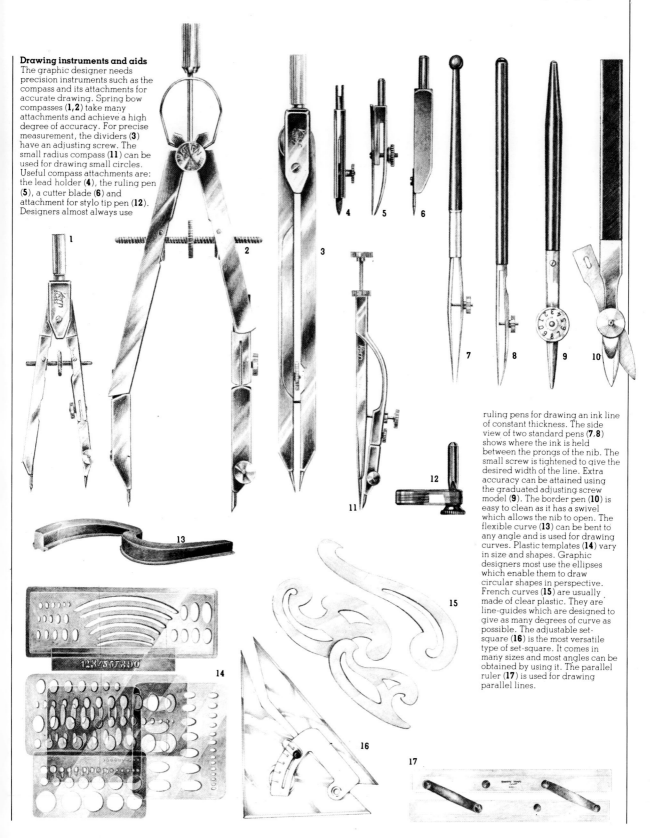

Drawing instruments and aids

The graphic designer needs precision instruments such as the compass and its attachments for accurate drawing. Spring bow compasses (**1,2**) take many attachments and achieve a high degree of accuracy. For precise measurement, the dividers (**3**) have an adjusting screw. The small radius compass (**11**) can be used for drawing small circles. Useful compass attachments are: the lead holder (**4**), the ruling pen (**5**), a cutter blade (**6**) and attachment for stylo tip pen (**12**). Designers almost always use ruling pens for drawing an ink line of constant thickness. The side view of two standard pens (**7,8**) shows where the ink is held between the prongs of the nib. The small screw is tightened to give the desired width of the line. Extra accuracy can be attained using the graduated adjusting screw model (**9**). The border pen (**10**) is easy to clean as it has a swivel which allows the nib to open. The flexible curve (**13**) can be bent to any angle and is used for drawing curves. Plastic templates (**14**) vary in size and shapes. Graphic designers most use the ellipses which enable them to draw circular shapes in perspective. French curves (**15**) are usually made of clear plastic. They are line-guides which are designed to give as many degrees of curve as possible. The adjustable set-square (**16**) is the most versatile type of set-square. It comes in many sizes and most angles can be obtained by using it. The parallel ruler (**17**) is used for drawing parallel lines.

Surfaces for the designer Most paper is available in the metricated 'A' sizes. Illustrated here are a selection of pads: the A2 pad of detail paper (**1**), A4 pads of tracing paper (**2.5**), A3 block of layout paper (**3**), A4 block of cartridge paper (**4**) and an A4 pad of graph paper (**6**). In addition to cartridge (**10**) and tracing paper (**8**), there is a wide range of paper which the graphic designer requires. For protecting artwork use a coloured paper called cover paper (**7**). For preparing roughs and layouts thin detail or layout paper is needed (**9**). Tracing down

paper (**11**) has a coloured backing. Acetate paper (**12**) is often used to protect dummy books or finished roughs. Kodatrace (**13**) and transparent adhesive paper (**14**) can both be used to protect artwork.

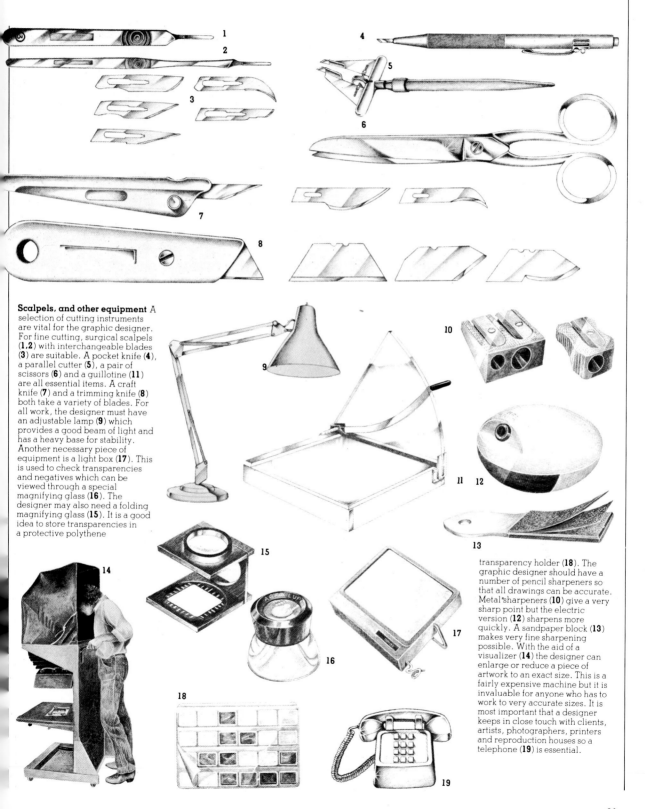

Scalpels, and other equipment A selection of cutting instruments are vital for the graphic designer. For fine cutting, surgical scalpels (**1,2**) with interchangeable blades (**3**) are suitable. A pocket knife (**4**), a parallel cutter (**5**), a pair of scissors (**6**) and a guillotine (**11**) are all essential items. A craft knife (**7**) and a trimming knife (**8**) both take a variety of blades. For all work, the designer must have an adjustable lamp (**9**) which provides a good beam of light and has a heavy base for stability. Another necessary piece of equipment is a light box (**17**). This is used to check transparencies and negatives which can be viewed through a special magnifying glass (**16**). The designer may also need a folding magnifying glass (**15**). It is a good idea to store transparencies in a protective polythene

transparency holder (**18**). The graphic designer should have a number of pencil sharpeners so that all drawings can be accurate. Metal sharpeners (**10**) give a very sharp point but the electric version (**12**) sharpens more quickly. A sandpaper block (**13**) makes very fine sharpening possible. With the aid of a visualizer (**14**) the designer can enlarge or reduce a piece of artwork to an exact size. This is a fairly expensive machine but it is invaluable for anyone who has to work to very accurate sizes. It is most important that a designer keeps in close touch with clients, artists, photographers, printers and reproduction houses so a telephone (**19**) is essential.

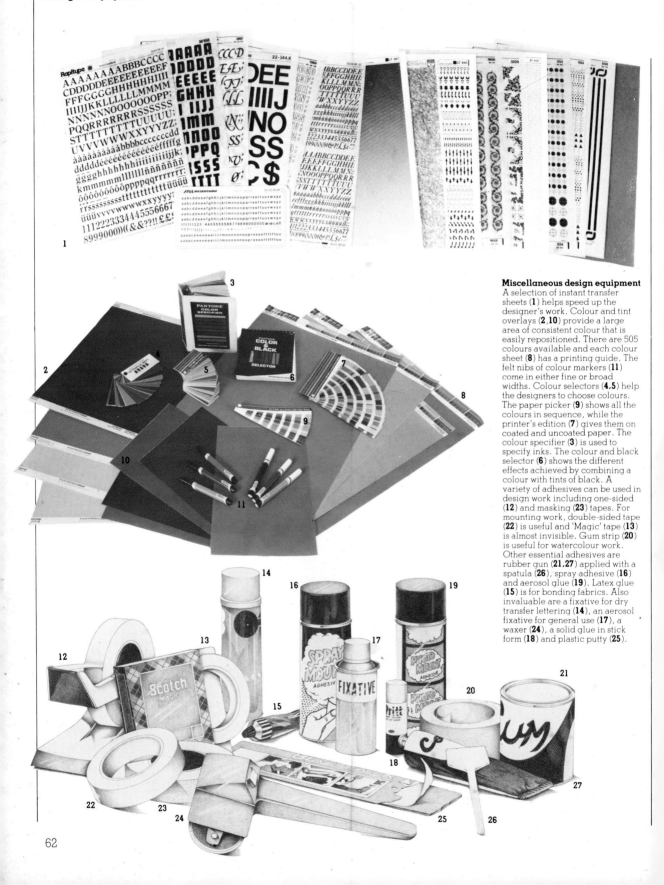

Miscellaneous design equipment
A selection of instant transfer sheets (**1**) helps speed up the designer's work. Colour and tint overlays (**2**,**10**) provide a large area of consistent colour that is easily repositioned. There are 505 colours available and each colour sheet (**8**) has a printing guide. The felt nibs of colour markers (**11**) come in either fine or broad widths. Colour selectors (**4**,**5**) help the designers to choose colours. The paper picker (**9**) shows all the colours in sequence, while the printer's edition (**7**) gives them on coated and uncoated paper. The colour specifier (**3**) is used to specify inks. The colour and black selector (**6**) shows the different effects achieved by combining a colour with tints of black. A variety of adhesives can be used in design work including one-sided (**12**) and masking (**23**) tapes. For mounting work, double-sided tape (**22**) is useful and 'Magic' tape (**13**) is almost invisible. Gum strip (**20**) is useful for watercolour work. Other essential adhesives are rubber gun (**21.27**) applied with a spatula (**26**), spray adhesive (**16**) and aerosol glue (**19**). Latex glue (**15**) is for bonding fabrics. Also invaluable are a fixative for dry transfer lettering (**14**), an aerosol fixative for general use (**17**), a waxer (**24**), a solid glue in stick form (**18**) and plastic putty (**25**).